THE CAPTAIN MYTH

THE RYDER CUP AND SPORT'S GREAT LEADERSHIP DELUSION

RICHARD GILLIS

BLOOMSBURY

LONDON · OXFORD · NEW YORK · NEW DELHI · SYDNEY

Bloomsbury Sport
An imprint of Bloomsbury Publishing Plc

50 Bedford Square
London
WC1B 3DP
UK

1385 Broadway
New York
NY 10018
USA

www.bloomsbury.com

BLOOMSBURY and the Diana logo are trademarks of
Bloomsbury Publishing Plc

First published 2016

© Richard Gillis, 2016

Richard Gillis has asserted his right under the Copyright, Designs and
Patents Act, 1988, to be identified as Author of this work.

British Library Cataloguing-in-Publication Data
A catalogue record for this book is available from the British Library.

Library of Congress Cataloguing-in-Publication data has been applied for.

UK ISBNs: HB: 978-1-4729-0994-7
TPB: 978-1-4729-0779-0
ePub: 978-1-4729-0781-3

US ISBNs: HB: 978-1-6204-0716-5
ePub: 978-1-6204-0718-9

2 4 6 8 10 9 7 5 3 1

Typeset in Adobe Garamond Pro by Deanta Global Publishing Services,
Chennai, India
Printed and bound in Great Britain by CPI Group (UK) Ltd, Croydon CR0 4YY

To find out more about our authors and books visit www.bloomsbury.com.
Here you will find extracts, author interviews, details of forthcoming events
and the option to sign up for our newsletters.

For Penny and Olivia

Contents

Prologue

'Be suspicious of the "because" and handle it with care'
Nassim Nicholas Taleb, The Black Swan

The Ryder Cup is one of the world's great sporting moments. Every two years the best golfers from America and Europe compete over three intense and emotionally charged days of high-quality sporting drama.

The event's global media profile has transformed the role of the team captain, who has become a major figure in the sporting landscape on both sides of the Atlantic, golf's contribution to the leadership industry, taking his place alongside the head coaches of the Major Leagues and the superstar managers of European football.

Yet the Ryder Cup captaincy doesn't easily fit the usual sports leadership template. He has limited input into the selection of his own team and he has no contractual authority over the players. The job is unpaid beyond generous expenses and he usually has little previous experience in a comparable role. Many of the team members are his direct peers – a group of highly skilled, highly motivated professionals at the very peak of their careers. Faced with this scenario, the traditional management levers of command and control have little relevance, making the role more nuanced and ambiguous than most.

Despite these apparent shortcomings, the captain is the lens through which we watch the event, his every decision parsed for meaning as we seek answers as to how to win the Ryder Cup, the all-important 'because'.

What type of leader is he, we wonder? Does he have an appetite for change, new ideas and a team of rookies? Or is he a steady-as-she-goes, don't-rock-the-boat merchant? Will he put his faith in the mercurial Flash Harry flop shot wizards or the men in grey and beige who play the percentage game and get the job done with no frills and frippery?

Then there's strategy. Will he go early with his big guns, or leave them to fight it out at the end? Should his pairings be based on technical factors like length and putting skill, or on personality? Does he divide them into pods or put their names in a hat? Should he do what Tony Jacklin did and play his best players in every session, or should he break up the stars and ensure everyone plays every day? Should he try to build a lead and hang on like Mark James, or rest his best players for Sunday like Davis Love? Then there's delegation: how many vice-captains does he need? Five like McGinley or one like Faldo? What about the course set-up? Should he trim the rough or let it grow, make the greens fast or slow? How does he motivate his team? Does he shout and holler, or put his arm around their shoulder? Will he send them out to battle with memorable quotes from great warriors, or remind them of their place in history with pictures on the walls of the team room? Should he get Sir Alex Ferguson to inspire his players or have President Bush read to them about the Alamo? Should he pray to God or Seve Ballesteros?

All of these questions are part and parcel of our enjoyment of the game, an attempt to make sense of what we see when the two teams come together. Ryder Cup history is divided into two over-arching storylines in which America's dominance has been overcome by the rise of Team Europe. Between 1927 and 1983, Team USA won 21 matches and halved one out of a total of 25, an 86 per cent winning record. Then, in 1985, Tony Jacklin led Europe to victory at the Belfry, inflicting the first defeat on America since 1957. Since that match, Europe has held sway: between 1985 and 2014 they won ten matches and tied one, a winning record of 70 per cent.

It follows that the stories we tell about the captains, the teams and the event itself must not only record the results – they must help make sense of them. These explanations are closer to myth than fact: assumptions that have no proven scientific basis, but which are commonly used as a version of the truth and which contrive to render the story of the event credible.

But winning the Ryder Cup can be misleading: the results often distort our analysis of what makes a good captain or a good team. This is because the only concrete evidence to support the winning captain's methods is the result. His team won, so we must find reasons for that victory. What he did must have worked. We won't accept that he did everything wrong and won, because that is a less coherent and satisfying story. Whoever heard of a bad winning captain?

This attribution error is rife throughout the debate on leadership in sport. The things we – fans, journalists, players, pundits – think contribute to Europe's success are often irrelevant.

The captain's made a decision *and* his team won. His team didn't win *because* of his decision. This mistake creates a series of myths, or delusions, the most prominent of which is the Captain Myth. When the winning putt is holed, two basic stories are given life.

The Good Captain story goes like this: Europe won because they were led by an inspirational person, whose strategy worked and whose partnerships clicked and whose team room was happier. The counter story is that America lost because of poor leadership by the Bad Captain. His pairings were ill conceived and his strategy was the wrong one. He wasn't helped by the bad blood in the team room or by the lack of team spirit. These stories are mere hearsay; the only evidence to support them is the result.

On top of these two basic myths – the Good and Bad Captain – are piled other delusions that add complexity. The Europeans, goes one argument, are more of a team than their American counterparts. The 'evidence' for this assumption is found in the smiles, the camaraderie and banter between team members, a view backed up by memories of European victories going back to the mid-1980s. Others elevate this explanation to a systematic issue, romanticising the European Tour as the scrappy underdog, whose best players came up the hard way, needing to win regularly to make a living. By contrast, goes this argument, the vast riches available even to journeymen on the PGA Tour had turned generations of American players soft and complacent, their true colours only revealed when the pressure of national pride is at stake. Yet others had seen a different match entirely. Their 'because' is a variant on that used to explain election results: it's the economy, stupid. The PGA Tour, like Wall Street and Silicon Valley, is a case study in globalisation. America has lost its competitive advantage in golf just as it has in the automobile industry, and the edge enjoyed by Team USA over the course of the American Century has gone for ever. Go back a generation or two and the American college system was hailed as the ultimate golfing production line. Since the 1980s, the same system is looked on with suspicion from those who see it as a hothouse for mediocrity: Rory McIlroy didn't need to go to college to become the best player in the world, runs the argument. Then, there are more technical answers to explain Europe's recent success: they are brought up playing more man-on-man matchplay, the format of the game tested at the Ryder Cup; they have an environmental advantage having played in difficult conditions on a more regular basis than their American counterparts; they play better in the wind because of exposure to seaside links courses and the Americans' superiority with the putter has been reduced due to advances in agronomy. And so on.

These stories remain in place, sometimes for years. Then, the results go a different way and the theories that seemed so watertight begin to leak. Every two years new ones are created and rolled into the melting pot of half-truths, conjecture, prejudice and superstition we refer to as Ryder Cup history. Their effect is widespread and not confined to the reputation of the individual captain; together they articulate each team's usable past and help shape their collective sense of identity. Their impact goes far beyond the psychological and they are often used as the basis of decision-making. This is how strategy evolves. What is deemed to have worked for one winning captain is passed down to the next until it becomes ingrained as the orthodoxy.

Yet, amid all this conjecture, one explanation – one myth – has been elevated above all others. The captain has become the single most important character in the story, our best guess at the all-important 'because'. But the rise of the captain is about far more than golf. It reflects our obsession with leadership, celebrity and a need for certainty and answers in a chaotic world.

The Captain Myth is not a self-help book. Its pages contain no secrets to a more successful career and a happier life, and it doesn't promise that by reading this book you'll become a great leader. Instead, it asks a different set of questions. Why do we so willingly buy into the cult of leadership in sport? What makes us grab at beguilingly simple explanations of triumph and defeat? Does the result of the match tell us anything useful about the link between the actions of the captain and the performance of his team? Do happier teams play better, or is team spirit just another error of attribution, a mistake we make in the rush to link cause and effect?

This book explains why we have come to view events such as the Ryder Cup through the lens of leadership and how we attribute credit and blame based entirely on the outcomes, creating cartoon versions of the Good and Bad Captain. Finally, *The Captain Myth* asks what the man in charge really represents and why we so willingly buy into the cult of the leader.

Chapter 1

The 1 Per Cent Putt

As Justin Rose settled over his ball on the 17th tee at Medinah, the story of the 39th Ryder Cup was falling into place.

After two days of highly competitive golf, Europe were four points down going into the final day's singles matches. Captain José María Olazábal's team had come out fighting on the final day but seemed to be coming up short, leaving Davis Love III destined to become only the second winning American Ryder Cup captain of the new millennium.

It was the culmination of three days of head-to-head competition between two teams of 12 of the best golfers from Europe and America. The players compete in 28 matches in all, each worth a point, with a ½ point awarded for drawn matches. The first team to reach 14½ points wins.

Like all the greatest sports events, the Ryder Cup matches often turn on tiny moments of inspired play, or outrageous luck. Nowhere was the tiny margin between victory and defeat better illustrated than in the match between Rose and America's Phil

Mickelson, who led their game by one point as the players walked from the 16th green to play the 17th hole.

At this moment in his career, Justin Rose had a pretty decent claim to be the best swinger of a golf club in the world. His action is a thing of beauty and is at its most efficient with the sort of shot that now faced him. Throughout 2012, Rose led the PGA Tour's Greens in Regulation category, the best indicator of a player's ball-striking consistency; of the top 125 players that year, nobody hit more greens from 150 to 225 yards. Of the 181 shots Rose hit in this range during competition that season, 141 finished on the green – 77.9 per cent. Medinah's 17th tee shot of 193 yards was smack in the middle of Rose's sweet spot.

The 17th poses a number of very difficult questions just as the pressure of competition is at its most intense, requiring a mix of excellent technique and mental strength, the perfect test of head and heart.

Between the tee and the green is the corner of Lake Kadijah, around which the Medinah Country Club was constructed. The 17th is designed so the lake dominates the player's view from the tee, cutting in along the front half of the green to the right. There is a diagonal cant that runs from front left to back right which creates two shallowed-out areas on either side of the green, which are the lowest points on the golf course. The flag was in its traditional final-day spot, positioned on the front right side of the green, tucked into a corner that reduces the margin of error between the water at the front and the bunker to the right.

To this is added the surprise element of wind. The tee sits back in a canopy of trees that shield the golfers as they play their shot. Only then does the wind come into play, hitting the ball as it leaves the shelter of the tee on its journey across the lake. The shot is downhill, playing further havoc with clubbing: often, players are hoodwinked into under-clubbing as the prevailing breeze hits the ball from the left, pushing it towards the bunker to the right of the green leaving the prospect of a near certain bogey four or worse. Too much club and you're faced with a chip from the rough above the green.

When he picked up his tee peg from the ground, Rose looked up and noted that he had done what he nearly always does when hitting an iron; he had hit the green.

Artists v Engineers

The differences between Phil Mickelson and Justin Rose are in reality very small. Mickelson has a reputation as having a better short game, while Rose's Greens in Regulation (GIR) stats give him the edge in terms of consistency with the longer clubs. Both hit the ball prodigious distances, Rose a little straighter, Mickelson slightly longer. Yet ask a golf fan who is the more talented player, and the answer will almost certainly come back as Phil Mickelson. Why this should be tells us something about how we view the role talent plays in golf.

To his legion of fans, Mickelson is a 'force of nature', 'blessed with God-given gifts'. This judgement is based on the brilliance of his wedges, his imaginative approach to recovery play and his greater appetite for risk. Despite his beautiful swing, Rose would generally be perceived to be less talented than Mickelson. In interviews he sometimes refers to himself as a 'grinder', which is golf speak for someone who has made the most of his ability, whose strength lies not in the flashy flop shots and outrageous recoveries, but in using his consistent swing to avoid trouble, to

3

find the fairway and then the green, to help him plot his way around the course, reducing the odds of failure. Greens in Regulation (GIR) is the grinder's badge of honour, and Rose is the best in the world in that category. GIR is about consistency. It reflects the meritocratic dream that you reap what you sow. 'The harder I practise the luckier I get,' said Gary Player, famously, which has become a sort of grinder's manifesto.

The perceived divide between Rose and Mickelson is between practice and talent. This runs through the game's history, separating great golfers of every generation into engineers and artists. At one end sit players whose appeal lies in the head more than the heart. Such a list might include Ben Hogan, Jack Nicklaus, Nick Faldo and Bernhard Langer. At the other end are the artists, the naturals, who inspire affection in addition to admiration: Walter Hagen, Sam Snead, Arnold Palmer and Seve Ballesteros would be included in this group.

The ability of the scientists seems more understandable to us, more within our grasp. In the deranged mind of the handicap golfer, there lies buried a belief that with access to the right coaches and equipment from a young age, they too could have been Justin Rose.

By comparison, even in their very wildest dreams, few people kid themselves that they could be Phil Mickelson. His game is not one that can be copied because we assume it is based on talent rather than just hours on the range. He is gifted with golf's great unquantifiables: feel and touch. It's in his fingers, we tell ourselves, and you can't teach that.

The fear often articulated by golfers of a certain age is that the artists are in retreat and science is winning. Players from across the world have levelled off in terms of playing style. The flying elbows and chicken-wing follow-throughs have been smoothed out by generations of coaches, each following the same curriculum. Where are the Irish swings, the peculiar Eamonn Darcy-like contraptions that used to populate every golf tour? Where are the players blessed with 'Spanish hands', the car park champions who can magic their way out of trouble with a flick of the wrist? In short, are we losing the romance?

It's a big issue for golf, says José María Olazábal. He says that sport, like business, faces a challenge to balance art and science, to use the data available to pursue excellence, whilst not losing the game's other essential element: creativity, which by definition is less easily quantifiable. 'They are two different worlds, it's true, but I would love to see them living together,' says Olazábal. 'We are losing part of one, the romantic part, the skill and the need for imagination. As players go looking for perfection we have all kinds of gadgets, all kinds of information, we can see our swings in video from four or five different angles, we can follow the path of the club, see how much the club is open or closed, on the backswing and at impact. So all that information is creating great players, great swings, it's true. But because of that, at the same time we are seeing less creative golf. We see more mechanical golfers, very accurate players, hitting fairways and greens in regulation. You see players rarely missing a shot on a round of golf, while in the past, because of the materials, a lack of preparation and, if you want, a lack of knowledge, we used to spread the ball more, we used to end up in different situations, in the trees, in the huge rough, in the car parks. We are losing that; it's true that I would love to see a combination of the two. When you look at Rory McIlroy's swing or Adam Scott's, or any of the young guys who are coming on the Tour now, the club is on the perfect path, they have huge speed through the ball, they are able to hit the ball 300-plus yards straight down the middle. That is fantastic, obviously. But we're losing the more eccentric, more individual swings of people like Jim Furyk, Lee Trevino or Raymond Floyd, whose strength lay in their imagination and flair. We will see fewer and fewer of those swings in the future. If we can get those two elements together that will be fantastic'.

A Change in the Odds

The closer Justin Rose gets to the green, the less effective he becomes, as his excellence with the longer clubs recedes and the importance of the short game increases. When compared to the very best players in the world, Rose is only an average putter. In 2012 Rose made just one from 103 putts of 25 feet or more during regulation Tour play, or 0.95 of a percentage point of putts made, placing him in 184th place on the PGA Tour in 2012.

Aware of his shortcomings, Rose had sought help from an unusual source. David Orr was a journeyman pro turned college teacher whose name had been passed to Rose by Sean Foley, his swing coach. 'There was an obvious frustration in Justin in playing tee-to-green better than anyone else but not getting the results,' said Orr. 'We had to figure what his tendencies were and build a plan. This isn't something lucky or magical or the product of some secret or tip from me.' Rose's biggest challenge is one that is common to virtually everyone who has played the game. 'His problem used to be missing to the right, and left-to-righters were particularly tough for him,' said Orr.

The left-to-right putt is the thing that keeps millionaire golfers up at night. It is what they talk about to their therapists and their swing doctors. The history of the game is littered with tournaments won and lost by a left-to-right putt. Golf's version of a snuff video is the grainy black and white footage of Doug Sanders missing a four-foot slider at St Andrews to lose the Open Championship in 1970. Bernhard Langer missed a ten-foot left-to-right to lose the 1991 Ryder Cup, and Europe's 2010 captain Colin Montgomerie still raves about the left-to-right putt made by Graeme McDowell to win at Celtic Manor. "That was downhill and about 25 feet from the hole. If that putt missed the story would have been very different. It didn't. It went in. From 25 feet away you generally hole fewer than 5 per cent of those. Downhill, left to right? We'd hole around 1 per cent of them. And it went in, right place, right time.'

Why this type of putt should be so difficult is open to conjecture. 'There's a dramatic difference between the number of right-to-left putts made versus left-to-righters,' Dave Pelz told the *New York Times* in 2011. 'At a distance of ten to 12 feet from the hole, handicap golfers miss three to four times as many left-to-righters as they do right-to-lefters.' In the late 1990s two university researchers, Tim Holman and Ed Stack, wrote a paper and then a book on the topic, concluding that the answer to problems with the left-to-right putt is to eliminate it altogether, preaching that players should 'switch-putt' – i.e. learn to putt left-handed when faced with the left-to-righter. Their work found favour at Stanford University, and was adopted by Notah Begay, a college teammate of Tiger Woods. Begay began switch-putting and took his game on to the PGA Tour, where he won four Tour events in 11 months running across 1999 and 2000 before back trouble limited his career.

Rose's solution to the slider problem was less technical, more psychological. He wanted to stop himself from overthinking and, instead, go back to the days of his childhood when putting was just something he did for fun. In 2010, Rose was asked to elaborate on this approach. 'I would say I'm doing it [freeing his mind] to about 80, 90 per cent,' said the Englishman. 'I still want to get better at it. It's what I'm trying to do. But being free is being fearless, not worrying about the consequences. And I guess it's taken a little hard work to get to that point. It's funny, that's how you play as a kid, and then the more and more you play PGA Tour golf or professional golf, the more that kind of clutter sticks to you, and it's a matter of trying to shake it all off. At the end of the day, it's a game, it's a golf course, and that's what you go out there to do − if you can break it down to that simple level, it makes the game easier; do you know what I mean? Obviously we play to win, but the challenge of winning is keeping it down to only the things you can control, and doing it better than everybody else.'

These mental gymnastics began to reap real benefits through the course of 2012. A couple of weeks before Medinah, at the 72nd hole of the Tour Championship in Atlanta, Rose was confronted with his nemesis, a 15-foot downhill left-to-right slider with $850,000 (£530,000) at stake. Rose holed it. 'That's where it all changed,' said David Orr. 'It's not just that Justin is putting well, but that he's putting well in the clutch moment.'

Advantage Lefty

By comparison to Justin Rose, Phil Mickelson's short game is a golfing phenomenon and the basis of a cottage industry. Any coach who can claim an association with Mickelson is fêted as the *guru de jour*. Since 2003 that role has been played mainly by Dave Pelz, a former NASA scientist who worked with Mickelson during a period that coincided with the player's first victory in a Major championship at the 2004 Masters.

Golfers are sport's hedge fund managers: they play a game in which tiny margins can represent massive amounts of money, and so the incentive to control any performance variable is higher in golf than in virtually any other sport. For this reason, Dave Pelz has found a warm welcome on the pro tours. Pelz's science story is backed up by a rigorous approach to the use of player performance data, a trend in which he was one of the pioneers. His research undermined a number of received wisdoms when it came to chipping and putting. He found that Tour professionals averaged about a 7 per cent error (or seven yards from the target per 100 yards) with clubs for which they used full swings, and that the error average was about 15 per cent with the full array of shorter wedge shots. This information led a small revolution in the way chipping and pitching were thought of by pro golfers. Terms such as 'touch' and 'feel' seemed outdated and unmeasurable in the light of Pelz's numbers. Players began to shape their practice to his findings, trying to apply the same consistency to chipping and pitching as they did to full swings. Partly on the back of Mickelson's first Major win at Augusta, Pelz became a putting-green celebrity, fronting DVDs, training aids and eventually a chain of branded short-game schools. It was Pelz who made Tom Kite the first 60-degree wedge to enable the Texan player to perform a full swing from shorter distances. Today, it's a rare professional golfer who doesn't carry at least three wedges in his bag. Mickelson sometimes packs four chipping clubs.

Pelz persuaded Mickelson to use his statistical data to help focus his practice sessions so they were shorter but more effective.

'As we work away from the hole, the percentage of putts made falls off exponentially,' Mickelson told NPR in 2013. 'So from three feet in, let's say I'm 100 per cent, when I move back one foot to four feet, that percentage falls to 88 per cent. And when I go another foot, to five feet, it falls to 75 per cent. And so on. This makes me focus my attention on my short game and chipping so that I'm working on getting each chip inside a three-foot circle.' Pelz encouraged Mickelson to practise by imagining a three-foot circle around the hole. 'If I can get it inside that circle, I know I'm going to make the next putt,' said the player.

At Medinah, in 2012, if Mickelson made birdie then Rose would have needed to hole his putt to halve the hole and take the game down the 18th. Mickelson would have been assured of at least half a point and American victory was all but secure.

From his position in the rough, the American played a beautiful low chip, the ball jumping from the longer grass at just the right pace to take the green's camber and roll towards the hole. Mickelson, and the crowd, thought it was in. The player walked along the edge of the first cut with his arm outstretched only to see the ball shave the hole, passing it by fractions of an inch on the high side. Had it gone in, the players would have been shaking hands and America almost certainly would have won the 2012 Ryder Cup.

Mickelson regained his composure and collected his ball for a gimme three, leaving Rose his monster putt for the hole.

For minutes Rose was crouched down on his haunches, like a quantity surveyor taking one last look at the contours of the earth before making a final decision. Moments later, the ball was on its way over the hog's back across the green before turning left to right. Rose remained in place as it disappeared into the middle of the hole, only then almost involuntarily lifting his putter. Mickelson stood and applauded as his opponent made the putt and then held up his thumb, turned to the crowd and encouraged them to applaud Rose's effort. Under the circumstances it was a very touching piece of sportsmanship.

Rose closed the match out down the 18th with another beautiful iron shot into the green followed by a clutch putt to make birdie as Mickelson's second overshot the green.

Later, Mickelson recognised that the drama on the 17th hole was pivotal to the result of the match: 'At 17, I thought I'd won the match, I thought I'd chipped in. I can't believe the ball didn't break that last inch in there. And after that ball didn't go in, he made that long putt. That was a huge momentum boost. What a big turnaround, because it looked like I was going to be dormie, if not close him out. On 18, when it looked like I might be able to stop some of the momentum on the board, they were able to get another point, and I thought that match, as early as it was, was a very pivotal one.'

Mickelson's analysis was shared by 2014 captain Tom Watson, who was more succinct when talking a year after Medinah: 'Rose misses and America wins the match, no doubt about it'.

Chapter 2

The Good Captain

If Justin Rose's 1 per cent putt was the moment when the match changed direction, it was a shorter putt by the German player Martin Kaymer that finally sealed Europe's unlikely victory. It came on the 18th green as Kaymer beat Steve Stricker to take Europe to the total of 14 points, the number required for them to retain the Cup. As holders, Europe only needed to draw the match to retain the Cup. This point became moot when the final match ended in a tie, giving Europe 14½ to USA's 13½.

As his ball went into the hole, Kaymer gave the world's media its money shot, the photograph that would run in the next day's papers. He punched the air and held both arms aloft before being engulfed by his teammates.

Europe's victory meant that Olazábal's leadership story had to be rewritten, and quickly. The perception that had grown up over the first two and a half days didn't fit the reality of Europe's win. During the week Olazábal had been painted as being an amiable but somewhat disengaged presence. In the face of America's onslaught, Olazábal's grip of events appeared to slip and he seemed to start second guessing his own strategy. Out went the idea to put the Swedish player Peter Hanson into the fray for the afternoon fourballs. This would have given Hanson an opportunity to make amends for his only previous match, a 5 and 4 defeat in Friday afternoon's fourball matches alongside Lee Westwood. But Olazábal was worried about Hanson. More specifically, it was the Swede's performance with the putter that was nagging away at the captain, who felt it might not be up to the mark on the lightning fast greens of Medinah Country Club. It was a tough call, but Olazábal decided to drop Hanson from the afternoon matches. The problem was, he didn't tell him. Rather, the Swede used the morning to play some practice holes with his caddie, noting down the tee positions in his course handbook and getting into what he called 'game mode'.

Olazábal's decision was relayed to the player just 20 minutes before he was due to tee off, as he was hitting putts on the practice green. 'I didn't take it very well, but I took it for myself,' said Hanson later. To his credit, he bottled his anger as best he could. 'I didn't let it go out over anyone else. I just locked myself in a dark room and stayed there for a couple of hours. I didn't damage the team, and that was the main thing.'

In isolation, Olazábal's handling of Hanson was clumsy but can't be held up as representative of his effectiveness as a leader. The next morning his critics were offered more ammunition when Rory McIlroy's time-keeping became one of the stories of Medinah and made a media star of Lombard deputy police chief Patrick Rollins, the policeman who drove the golfer through the streets of suburban Chicago after he claimed to have misread the time.

Thinking that his match started at 12.25 p.m., McIlroy was still at the team's Westin hotel in Lombard, around half an hour from the Medinah Country Club. 'We have a point person who has been co-ordinating the Lombard side of things, and all the players had left the hotel and no one had seen Rory,' said Rollins.

The Irishman's mistake was only picked up when a few of the courtesy vehicle drivers mentioned they hadn't seen McIlroy, who then received panicked calls from the course. 'I read the tee times on my phone and they are obviously on Eastern time, and it's Central time here,' McIlroy told reporters that afternoon. Rollins said the golfer looked stunned, anxious and like 'a lot was going through his mind'. The policeman checked whether McIlroy suffered from motion sickness before setting off. McIlroy, a keen Formula 1 fan, replied, 'No, just get me there. Get me there.'

The film of McIlroy arriving at the clubhouse, sandwich in hand, was beamed around the world. When he, and Europe, subsequently won the match, the story was played out as a comedy. Had they lost, it would have been given a different spin. As it was, few bothered to question how such a mistake could have been allowed to happen, and whether Team Europe was quite the well-oiled machine it is routinely painted as.

The slipshod nature of McIlroy's escapade allied with the handling of Peter Hanson and the decision to rest Ian Poulter, Luke Donald and Sergio García on Friday afternoon meant that a broader narrative was forming in the minds of fans and the media. If Europe was going to lose for only the second time in the new millennium, then someone had to pay. That man was the captain, that's what he's (not) paid for. However, Olazábal was spared this write-up by the scintillating golf his team played late on the Saturday afternoon and through the Sunday singles.

Magical Thinking

After Rose's 1 per cent putt had fallen into the hole, Olazábal's captaincy was given a more positive spin. Almost immediately, the component parts to his captain myth were put into place. The nature of Europe's comeback lent Olazábal's leadership an otherworldly air, and there was talk of magic in the air. 'Ollie said to us that the Ryder Cup is what memories and dreams are made of, and last night that team room was buzzing,' said Ian Poulter at the post-match press conference. 'We weren't four points down. We felt like we were all square. We just knew we had a chance. And do you know this is history right here.'

Poulter referenced the team kit organised by Olazábal for the Sunday singles that paid homage to the navy blue and white ensemble worn by Ballesteros at the 1984 and 1988 Open Championships: 'We knew Ollie had us wearing Seve's navy blue and white for a reason. We had Seve on our bags, on our shirts and in our hearts. We did this for Seve.'

Sergio García felt the same way. 'We did believe,' he said. 'There's no doubt that we've been inspired by Seve, through our captain. I don't know how my teammates pulled it off. I got a little bit lucky today, but I found something. There was no chance I would have won my match if he wasn't up there looking down on me.'

Ever since Olazábal had been confirmed as captain, he had been at pains to pay tribute to his great friend and fellow Ryder Cup hero, who was a defining figure in European golf over four decades. Ballesteros won five Major championships, helped popularise golf in Europe and in particular, revelled in the passion of the Ryder Cup's biennial battle with the United States. From their first meeting at a pro-am in Spain, Ballesteros had taken a brotherly interest in Olazábal's development as a professional golfer, and the two men had much in common. They were both brought up around golf courses in northern Spain. Their partnership in Ryder Cup matches began at Muirfield Village in 1987, when Europe won in America for the first time. Ballesteros and Olazábal, Seve and Ollie, were to amass the best points record of any partnership in the event's history, forming the bedrock of the successful Europe teams of that era. Together the Spanish pair played 15 matches, winning 11, halving two, losing two. The great man's premature death in 2011 aged just 54 was as heartbreaking as it was cruel.

Olazábal was acutely aware of the legacy of Ballesteros on the next generation of golfers. He recounted a story from his first Ryder Cup in 1987: 'It was the first day and I was obviously shaking like a leaf because I'd never seen such crowds, you know, people on both sides of the fairway, shouting and clapping. I left the putting green and walked towards the tee, which was 30 yards away. Seve approached me and he walked beside me all the way to the tee, and he looked at me and said, "José, you just play your game and I will take care of the rest." So, in a way, he took a lot of responsibility away from me. It told me that I could rely on him: "Whatever he does, I am just going to concentrate on my game."

'On the golf course you have to be yourself, it doesn't matter if it is the Ryder Cup or not, you have to play your game,' said Olazábal. 'No one knows your game better than yourself, and somehow you have to play as freely as possible, and that's very difficult to achieve, especially under those circumstances. And for the captain it is very important to transmit that information to the players; the captain is going to be there to back them up whatever happens.'

To give Olazábal's story greater credibility, the media went in search of a guru, in the shape of teamwork expert Khoi Tu, 'a man who has advised Formula 1 champions and some of the world's leading companies'. Tu took the Seve factor and ran with it, suggesting that it was the difference between the two teams. 'Teams are often at their best when playing for an idea,' said Tu, whose book *Superteams* was published shortly after Medinah. 'I'm not sure the US did a lot wrong. But since the contest was so close, the key differentiator could be the "Seve" idea.'

This reading of Europe's win fitted perfectly with the events we'd seen unfold before our eyes. The explanation being put forward was a combination of fact – Europe won from four points down – with guesswork: Europe's superior team spirit was the deciding factor, with the ghost of Seve as the catalyst. 'Like most sports, golf is a combination of will and skill and at this level,' said Khoi Tu, 'the will is often more important than the skill.'

The Enigmatic Basque

The secret to a leadership myth is distillation: taking something as complex and messy as a human being and simplifying them, using only the parts of the personality that are useful to the story and discarding the parts that run counter to it. The captain's story combines his known or assumed personality traits with some broad national stereotypes and biographical detail. This cartoon version of the captain is then planted into the timeline of the match to help explain basic cause and effect. Perhaps more than any captain in recent times, José María Olazábal resists this process.

He lives in the small hillside village of Fuenterrabía, a short drive from the coastal city of San Sebastián on Spain's north coast. A narrow tree-lined avenue off the main road leads to the entrance to the Real Golf Club de San Sebastián. The clubhouse is an elegantly rustic building surrounded by a walled courtyard. The vibe is one of understated affluence, populated by the sort of well-dressed Europeans who dominate the imagination of Englishmen on their summers abroad: greying, middle-aged men wearing pastel colours with absolute confidence; Lacoste and cashmere, loafers without socks, tanned ankles. The Real is José María Olazábal's home club. He was born there and still lives in a house just off the 12th fairway.

The reasons Olazábal is universally popular are those that make him harder to caricature. He lacks the comedy bombast of a Colin Montgomerie or Seve Ballesteros. He can appear distant at times, wrapped in his own thoughts. Even that old standby, national stereotype, doesn't help much. When pushed to describe a typical Basque, Olazábal's explanation just made him sound more enigmatic: 'Basque people are very hard to get to know, you have to coax them out of their shell at first, but once you get through the shell, you have a friend for life. I am pretty much that way. It's very hard for anyone to really get close to me at first, but if he earns my confidence and friendship he will be a friend for the rest of my life.'

Olazábal is great value as an interviewee. Honest, funny, warm and insightful, and very aware of the absurdity at the heart of this little venture. He knew full well that but for Justin Rose's putt,

Sergio García's bunker shot, Steve Stricker's putting woes and a hundred other individual moments over that weekend in September 2012, it would be Davis Love's opinion that we'd now be seeking.

He was right, of course. It's idiotic to define a leader's impact on his team in terms of simple cause and effect. It follows that it makes no sense to explain what happens in any Ryder Cup solely through the lens of the winning captain. Sport, like life, is far more complex than that. But the captain myth rejects complexity in favour of a good tale. 'When the legend becomes fact, print the legend,' said John Ford. So Olazábal was turned into a leadership case study and took his place among the Good Captains of the recent past.

Passionate Celts and Efficient Germans

In 2006, Ian Woosnam captained Europe to a crushing victory over Tom Lehman's side at the K Club in Ireland. The location helped form the Good Captain narrative of the fiery Welshman who drank Guinness with his fellow Celts as Europe overwhelmed Team USA.

In the run up to the K Club, Paul McGinley gave a picture-perfect description of the Passionate Celt to the media: 'Ian Woosnam has a great affinity with the people of Ireland and it's not just because he is a twice champion of the Irish Open. Woosie is a born winner who is passionate about his sport. The Irish idolise their determined and successful sportsmen so Woosie will have instant respect and adulation. But what will endear him to the people of Ireland even more is the fact that Woosie loves the craic. After a hard day's work, Woosie loves nothing more than going into the bar to relax with a few pints of Guinness for a chat with whoever's around. The Irish take to that attitude – they don't take kindly to prima donnas. So in that sense he'll be a real people's captain and a hugely popular one at that. After all, Woosie is one of our Celtic cousins.'

In recent years the Passionate Celt has been occupied in varying guises by Sam Torrance in 2002 and Colin Montgomerie at Celtic Manor in 2010. Go back a generation or two and he reappears as Dai Rees, Brian Huggett, Bernard Gallacher and Eric Brown, the 1969 captain, a man rarely mentioned in Ryder Cup history books without the word 'combative' attached.

In contrast to the Passionate Celt, the Efficient German is a tale of head over heart. Bernhard Langer occupies a position at the science end of golf's spectrum. His role in Team Europe has been to play the hard-working engineer to the lovable but flaky artists from Ireland and southern Europe. The most often repeated story about Bernhard Langer is of him asking his caddie Pete Coleman for yardages from either side of the water-sprinkler head when preparing to hit from the fairway. The player and his caddie both deny this ever happened, but that's beside the point. It's enough that it feels true. He is what he calls a '2–3 handicap skier' yet only skis at Christmas in order that he has recovery time before the season starts should something untoward happen. Those seeking to emphasise his mental toughness point out that he has won three times in the week after a Ryder Cup, including 1991, when it was his putt on the final green that cost the team the Cup.

When his time came to lead in 2004, write-ups of Langer's Good Captain story were peppered with phrases that linked him to the production values of German car makers. This post-match account was typical: 'Langer was word perfect as he explained his strategy. His players spoke of their captain's attention to detail, his understanding of partnerships, the chemistry within the team and his careful use of the debutants. Rookies Ian Poulter, Paul Casey and David Howell spent the opening day getting used to the atmosphere. They saw a partisan American crowd muted by European golf played with a smiling but ruthless efficiency that produced the biggest opening-day lead ever by a visiting Continental team.'

Langer's victory was enough to place him alongside other notable sports coaches known for their attention to detail, such as England rugby coach Sir Clive Woodward, Bill Belichick of the New England Patriots and Sir Dave Brailsford, Team GB's cycling supremo. The cool, calculating German was not just a product of media coverage. It was how many of the players chose to define him. This is Colin Montgomerie's description of that 2004 match: 'There wasn't the passion of some of his predecessors, just magnificent efficiency . . . while he was in charge you felt that nothing had been left to chance, everything had been carefully thought out.' *Vorsprung durch technik*, as they say in German car advertising.

The Efficient German and the Passionate Celt have alter egos that are ready to appear when things go wrong. At the K Club, Ian Woosnam's alter ego was lurking in the shadows, lying in wait, ready to flip the skipper's 'fiery Welsh passion' into something darker. It's a short jump from passion to ill discipline and if he had lost, Woosie's famed 'love of the craic and a pint of Guinness' would have been interpreted differently too. 'I couldn't believe how much they drank,' said Steve Pate after watching Team Europe drown their sorrows at Kiawah Island in 1991. It's worth noting that one American term for alcoholism is 'the Celtic

Disease'. Likewise, the captain myth demands that Bernhard Langer's story take a different turn had Europe lost at Oakland Hills in 2004. No doubt the captain's legendary attention to detail would have been seen differently. The other side of 'Germanic efficiency' is humourlessness, distance and lack of empathy.

For a glimpse of what might have been, Langer and Woosnam need only note the kicking meted out to Davis Love at Medinah.

Chapter 3

The Bad Captain

In contrast to Europe, Team USA's poor Ryder Cup record means that their recent history is viewed mainly through the lens of the Bad Captain. Hal Sutton's reputation has never recovered from the experience of losing in 2004. The defeat cemented Sutton's place in Ryder Cup history as the simple-minded redneck who was outsmarted by the superior intellect and organisational rigour of Bernhard Langer, the Efficient German.

Sutton is remembered for two things: he wore a cowboy hat and paired the two best players in the world – Tiger Woods and Phil Mickelson – on the first day.

The hat became the motif of his Bad Captain story. 'For yesterday morning's start of the Ryder Cup, Sutton, a Louisiana horseman, showed up in a cowboy hat,' ran the next day's piece in the *Philadelphia Inquirer*. When his team trailed 6½ to 1½ after day one, Sutton was asked if the hat was going to make a reappearance. 'Oh, yeah, we're going to have a team meeting,' said Sutton. 'I'm going to have to put that cowboy hat back on. This time, I may get out the reins, too, and make them wet.'

The poor performance of his team encouraged the media to turn Sutton into a cartoon cowboy, a version of Homer Simpson in a Stetson. Before the match a British journalist labelled Sutton 'J. R. Ewing without the brains and the ten gallon hat.' When the match went against Team USA Sutton wore the hat again, prompting the same reporter to have another go. 'Unfortunately for him [Sutton] and the American team he was supposed to be guiding, the brains never showed up.'

For Tom Lehman and Corey Pavin, losing captains in 2006 and 2010 respectively, their religious faith became the stick with which they were beaten. Lehman's captaincy was framed through the lens of the evangelical preacher and was a clear example of the captain myth being projected onto the team as a whole; several accounts referred to that 2006 team as 'his flock'. *Sports Illustrated* suggested there was 'a religious undercurrent to this American team', an interpretation that was given greater credence when Lehman chose two fellow born again Christians, Stewart Cink and Scott Verplank as his wildcard picks. The *Wall Street Journal* reported that golf legend Byron Nelson, an accomplished woodworker, made a small wooden keepsake for each player with a verse from *Psalms* on one side, and that some of the players had Christian fish symbols on their bags.

Corey Pavin, the 2010 captain, was born Jewish but converted to Christianity in 1991 and, like Lehman, is a member of the Fellowship of Christian Athletes, a group that wields considerable power in American school and college sport. The group's mission statement talks of challenging coaches and athletes on the professional, college, high school, junior high and youth levels 'to use the powerful medium of athletics to impact the world for Jesus Christ. FCA focuses on serving local communities by equipping, empowering and encouraging people to make a difference for Christ.'

Talking to the American journalist Bruce Selcraig, the former European Ryder Cup player turned TV commentator David Feherty famously said that Europeans found evangelical Christians as 'frightening as conservative Muslims'. Feherty's remark was just one high profile media moment among many and it reflected the shift in the way the captain and the American team were being viewed.

The experience of Lehman and Pavin highlighted how coverage of the captaincy had evolved. No longer just a reason for losing the Ryder Cup, the captain had become a repository for anti-American sentiment. Since the 1980s, when the matches became closer, the personalities and background of the captain and the players have been used to put clear water between the teams. 'Let us be painfully honest about it,' wrote British columnist Matthew Norman after America won at Brookline in 1999. 'Yes, they are repulsive people, charmless, rude, cocky, mercenary, humourless, ugly, full of nauseatingly fake religiosity, and as odious in victory as they are unsporting in defeat.'

Such coverage reflected a change in the way America was being viewed that went far beyond the golf course and the Ryder Cup. The writer Barbara Ehrenreich developed this theme. Central to American nationalism – a core American sense of identity – has been the belief that the US is 'the greatest nation on earth', wrote Ehrenreich. Americans, she said, tend to define themselves as more dynamic, democratic and prosperous. Religious leaders on the Christian right, a key constituency of American Ryder Cup teams, like to buttress this conceit with the notion that Americans are 'God's chosen people' and politicians of every stripe routinely describe their country as 'the leader of the free world'.

This brand of American triumphalism was ever-present throughout the era before 1985, often surfacing at the traditional pre-match speeches made by the captains. In 1967 Ben Hogan made one of the shortest and most devastating captain's speeches on record. Hogan sat impassively at the top table as Great Britain captain Dai Rees took an age to introduce his team, talking them up one by one as the audience sat and stared back at him in near silence. When Rees finally sat down, Hogan asked his American side to stand: 'Ladies and Gentlemen, the United States Ryder Cup team – the finest golfers in the world.'

This was hardly controversial given the talent Hogan had at his disposal: Arnold Palmer, Doug Sanders, Billy Casper and Julius Boros were just a handful of the Major winners in that side. 'The British were two down before a ball had been hit,' said Peter Alliss. When Europe began winning under Tony Jacklin in the eighties, America's triumphalism began to sound more forced. Europe's run of victories from 1985 to 1989 had disrupted the equilibrium of the match, undermining previous certainties. European players were no longer the natural underdogs, a fact that American golfers seemed reluctant to accept.

The historian Godfrey Hodgson noted a shift in how America was being viewed around the world. American exceptionalism was 'once idealistic and generous, if somewhat solipsistic' and had now evolved into something altogether less appealing. The reporting of the Ryder Cup merely reflected this change in attitudes. The 1990s opened with the War on the Shore in 1991 and closed at the Battle of Brookline in 1999. The version of America represented by Arnold Palmer and Jack Nicklaus gave way to something harder, less congenial, and anti-American sentiment began to bleed into some of the more extreme coverage.

In 1991, American captain Dave Stockton led Team USA to a one-point victory at Kiawah Island. His Good Captain narrative is a version of *Hogan's Heroes*: the gun-toting outdoorsman leading a team of khaki-wearing mercenaries to redemption. The military connotations that accompany both the match and the captain come from a number of sources, in particular the timing of the event, which came shortly after the end of the first Gulf War.

The marketing department of the PGA of America created a clips video to be shown at the pre-match dinner, entitled *War on the Shore*, which quickly became the event's central theme. 'If it's a war they want, let's give them one,' said Nick Faldo, one of many European players who was left bemused by the video's airbrushing of European success from Ryder Cup history.

The choice of golf course was another factor. The Ocean Course at Kiawah Island is in an area that also features a number of American military installations. Stockton issued camouflage hats to his troops, which became potent symbols of the event and Stockton's captain myth. Most famously, the hats were worn on Saturday afternoon by Corey Pavin and Steve Pate in their defeat to Bernhard Langer and Colin Montgomerie. The image of Pavin in camouflage has since defined the player in the eyes of European golf fans. In his own defence, Pavin said he wore the hat to show camaraderie with returning soldiers from the Gulf. 'They could have worn something to support their troops if they wanted,' said

Hale Irwin, years later. 'British troops wear camo, too. Last I heard, they don't wear bright-yellow jumpsuits.'

The level of aggression at Kiawah was an early sign of things to come. 'The Europeans had been better than us, and they weren't shy about reminding us,' said Paul Azinger. 'The British media especially weren't bashful about letting us know about that. But in 1991 we had a new wave of young, terrific players who were also patriotic. Payne, me, Pavin and Pate especially, along with warriors like Raymond, Lanny, Hale and Stockton as captain. We didn't like having our noses rubbed in it, and we took it kind of personally.'

Stockton has since said he is embarrassed by the war connotations of Kiawah and prefers to remember a moment after the post-match dinner, when the two teams shared the bus back to the hotel. He recalls Ian Woosnam inviting the American team onto the European bus: 'Woosie said, "Stock, we can get everybody on, we're only two people shy." And with that he picks up Corey Pavin and carries him on the bus so he counts as one person.'

Such moments of camaraderie don't fit the Kiawah narrative, however, which is based on conflict. 'I stirred up a hornet's nest,' said Stockton later, 'but I don't care.' The Ryder Cup needs hornets he said, otherwise the Americans 'get complacent' and the whole event loses its edge.

Patriotism is a card that America has that Europe cannot match, says José María Olazábal. 'The Americans are very proud of themselves, of the country they live in. Their flag means a lot to them. They are very intense when they have to defend their country or their image. And in that regard, the Ryder Cup makes them really fight hard for it, and they are very proud of that.' But Stockton was not the first or last American captain to evoke the American flag and use patriotism to motivate his team.

Love's Story

In the hours following Medinah, Davis Love's Bad Captain story was altered to reflect America's defeat. This was challenging because the view until midway through Sunday was that Love had played a blinder. His team's victory would upend the clichés that had grown up around Team USA over the last three decades. The received wisdom was that they were a bunch of selfish loners, who played for themselves and for money above all, and who were found wanting when it came to the team version of the sport; where Europe's players were inspired by the nationalistic fervour of the Ryder Cup, the Americans were hobbled by it. Europeans were more natural matchplayers, street fighters able to adapt better to the event's matchplay, man-on-man format.

Leading by four points on Saturday evening, it was America who seemed to be coming together as a unit. Tearing up that narrative was going to be tough. It would need details.

Two decisions left Love vulnerable. Firstly he'd benched Mickelson and Keegan Bradley on Saturday afternoon. This was later used to explain the European fightback, led by Ian Poulter. A harder man than Love would have kept his boot on the throat of the opponent.

As with every captain, Love's other weak spot was his wildcard picks, which came back to haunt him. He went with experience – Steve Stricker and Jim Furyk – over youthful potential – Rickie

Fowler and Hunter Mahan. The rationale was sound enough, the only problem with the theory was that both Stricker and Furyk lost their singles matches at key moments.

How much defeat at Medinah mattered to Davis Love can be gauged by the contents of a letter he wrote to an American publisher in the hours after the match. 'I should be tired but I'm not,' he wrote. 'We lost the Ryder Cup about six hours ago, and now I'm at the team hotel, a Westin in suburban Chicago, trying to make sense of what just happened.' His team had dispersed. Tiger Woods had texted on the way to the airport. There were wrong turns and construction traffic, the city's road system was jammed with people trying to make their way home after the Miracle at Medinah. 'A perfect ending to a perfect day,' was Tiger's message. 'I'm going to carry this defeat with me for the rest of my life,' wrote Love. 'The biggest part of the captain's job is to win, and I lost.'

Many of Love's decisions had paid off. The four-point lead on Saturday night was due to some clever use of pairings. 'Man, that Keegan Bradley is on fire,' said Freddie Couples, Love's assistant captain on Saturday morning. 'Ride him all the way to the house.' Play him and Phil Mickelson on Saturday afternoon was the message. Don't let any light in, give 'em nothing; once the momentum is with you, take full advantage. Love's plan had involved playing each of the two-man teams that had been established before arriving at Medinah three times over the course of the first four sessions. 'Golfers tend to be creatures of habit. We like order. I was trying to provide order.' Mickelson had told Love he was tired on Saturday, and wanted to keep himself ready for the singles on Sunday. 'There was no reason to play Keegan with a partner with whom he had not practised,' wrote

Love. 'There was no reason to mess with order. Things were going according to plan.'

When he went to the press room that evening, a fierce interrogation of his leadership began in earnest. The starting point was Love's wildcard picks, every captain's most vulnerable point. Paul Azinger's success in the 2008 Cup persuaded Love to keep the formula his predecessor had created. His selection of Dustin Johnson was beyond criticism. The long-hitting player from South Carolina won three points from the three matches he played, but Jim Furyk and Brandt Snedeker were less impressive, managing just a point each from their week's work.

The press sensed blood in Love's faith in Steve Stricker, the 45-year-old self-styled grinder who had hitherto found a niche for himself in the role of partner to Tiger Woods. Stricker lost to Martin Kaymer on the final hole, handing the German his big media moment, the putt to keep the Ryder Cup. Kaymer held up his hands for that photo that went around the world, before running into the arms of his teammates and leaving Stricker to slouch off the green nursing a 0–4 record for the week.

He, along with Furyk, 42, were selected to add grit to the team and be a calming influence. They were the safe choices for the 48-year-old American captain who knew their games intimately from years of playing with them as their direct contemporary on the PGA Tour.

'In my experience, experience is overrated,' said Mark James, the 1999 European captain, who took the greenest team ever to play a Ryder Cup to Brookline and nearly won. What use is experience if it is experience of losing? Ryder Cup defeat has been the norm for Stricker's generation of American golfers: just two American teams had won since 1993.

There is something deeper here too. By giving Love four picks, the captain was given responsibility for choosing a third of the team, leaving eight to play their way onto the team. This seemed to go against something in the American psyche, namely that merit should be earned and that the opportunity to represent your country should not be gifted to friends, rather it should be a shoot-out between battle-hardened players desperate to play themselves onto the team. This is certainly Tom Watson's view; the 2014 captain felt that the 'purest form' of Ryder Cup selection would be no wildcard picks at all. Raymond Floyd was the first American captain to be given wildcard picks, in 1989, the PGA of America's response to back-to-back defeats in 1985 and 1987. 'Maybe that's the way we should go back to,' Watson said at Gleneagles a year on from the 2014 match. 'I reduced my picks from four to three, and was thinking actually two because I wanted the players who were playing to get on the team to have that as a goal. And if they got there, then they've earned something very, very special. Maybe we should go back to that. If you really look at it, the purest form of Ryder Cup would be no captain's picks, 12 players who qualify,' Watson said. 'That's the way I qualified.'

The criticism of Love didn't stop with team selection, however. It quickly moved to his line-up for the Sunday singles matches and, in particular, the decision to load the bottom of the order with what he called 'Steady Eddies' – Furyk, Stricker and Tiger Woods – three players who finished the week with a combined score of 2–8–1.

To this was added the decision to rest Mickelson and Bradley on Saturday afternoon. They had been brilliant all week and, what's more, won so easily that their matches had finished early.

Over the first three sessions their workload consisted of just 44 holes from a possible 54.

Like a boxing trainer saving his man from too much punishment, Phil Mickelson stepped in to divert the questions away from Love, putting his hand over the microphone to interrupt: 'Hold on one sec, Davis,' said Mickelson. 'As far as playing Keegan and I, you need to hear something. Keegan and I knew going in that we were not playing in the afternoon, and we said on the first tee, "We are going to put everything we have into this one match, because we are not playing the afternoon." And when we got to ten, I went to Davis and I said, "Listen, you're seeing our best. You cannot put us in the afternoon, because we emotionally and mentally are not prepared for it. And I know you're going to get pressure, because we're playing so good. But we have other guys that are dying to get out there, and we have mentally put everything into this match. We won't have anything later, and so you need to stay to our plan."'

Mickelson's speech was an act of kindness, an attempt to save his friend further punishment and to rescue his reputation as a captain. 'Our plan' had a ring to it. This wasn't something done in isolation, was the message, it was a team decision. We live and die together. Love's face, however, could not conceal the truth that he knew his fate. Two years of planning and strategising, of studying player form and nursing huge egos, had come to nothing. He had lost and there was nothing he nor Mickelson could do to alter that.

'One of the big things at Medinah was why did we make the 17th hole such a tough pin placement,' says Freddie Couples. 'That was a big question mark, we lost the 17th hole in every match that went through there, regardless of whether Justin Rose makes a 40-footer or not. Every match we lost. We also lost the third hole, the seventh hole, the 11th hole. That was brought up in the post-match meetings'.

Ultimately the buck stopped with the Bad Captain. 'If you need to blame somebody for this loss, blame me,' he wrote later. 'I'm the one who signed off the Sunday line-up, for the 12 singles matches.' Europe won eight of the 12 and tied one. The putts that dropped on the first two days dried up, and even switched sides. 'It wasn't for lack of trying. Too much trying, if anything. José María was suffering like I was. He was wind-whipped, his face was lined and his eyes were red. I'm glad I couldn't see myself.'

'All day Sunday, I still thought we were going to win,' said Love, interviewed two months later. 'We just needed a few guys to finish it off. Somewhere around five o'clock I finally realised, "Holy cow, they're not finishing it off." That's when it went bad. I knew going in, the narrative was either going to be the team won or the captain screwed it all up. And ultimately I didn't get them to calm down on Sunday. That's on me; that's coaching.'

'What could I have done differently?' asked Love, posing the question encountered by every leader in any sphere, from sport to politics and business: do I matter?

Chapter 4

Why We Fall for the Captain Myth

The experience of José María Olazábal and Davis Love mirrors that of every leader in any sphere, from sport to politics and business, who routinely get too much credit and too much blame for events beyond their control.

The captains are subject to what social scientists call a fundamental attribution error, a variation of which is given the label of leadership attribution bias. In this case, we tend to overweight the effect that a leader has on different outcomes, whether we are voting for the president, selecting the next chief executive or calling for a football manager's head. When these psychological biases are meshed with our obsession with celebrity, it's easy to understand how the captain has become such a prominent figure in the sports world.

Following his team's victory at Gleneagles in 2014, Paul McGinley was the latest Good Captain to be welcomed into the leadership industry, a business sector estimated to be worth in the region of $50 billion. There are over 400 accredited business schools in America alone, and many more around the world, each teaching a curriculum driven by thousands of leadership experts, many of whom make a very decent living writing, speaking and teaching the fundamentals of this relatively new topic. The subject is of intense interest to the government and the military, and to the corporate sector, which ploughs large sums of money into developing its own centres of excellence, running courses, seminars and workshops, and putting company names to leadership institutes and think tanks.

The Good Captain is part of a new generation of head coaches, managers and performance directors from the world's most famous teams and franchises. The profile of Major League head coaches and European football managers transcends that of most of their players, and strategy has become their mantra. This is sport's knowledge economy, in which coaches do the thinking and players are relegated to the position of pieces on a chess board.

'Leadership' is the buzzword of our times, wrote the author David Foster Wallace. 'Its meaning has been forcibly squeezed out of them by regurgitative overuse and relentless over-application to things that increasingly dilute the essence of the concept the word once used to capture. In a culture that calls pop culture celebrities "thought-leaders" and looks for "leadership ability" in kindergartners, we're left wondering what leadership actually means and questioning what makes a great leader.'

Yet despite huge investment in the subject, the leadership industry has largely failed to deliver much evidence that attributes the actions of leaders to the performance of their organisations. In 1985 respected academic James R. Meindl wrote a seminal research paper called 'The Romance of Leadership', which concluded that the actions of the chief accounted for no more than 15 per cent of the variation in the company's performance.

Businesses, like sports teams, succeed or fail due to many factors, or as Professor Henry Mintzberg put it, the 'interplay of social, economic and other impersonal forces that shape and constrain even the most heroic individual efforts'. By focusing on the single person, said Mintzberg, 'leadership becomes part of the syndrome of individuality' that is undermining organisations. 'By the excessive promotion of leadership, we demote everyone else.'

The experience of the Ryder Cup captain is an extreme example of the halo effect, something first identified by American psychologist Edward Thorndike in the 1920s. Thorndike noted our tendency to make 'specific inferences on the basis of a general impression' and it is rife across the business and political spectrum, and has bled into professional sport. When a company is doing well the business press and stock market analysts make up stories to explain the success. The effect must have a cause so they point to the way the company is run and assume it is led by competent people employing a winning strategy. If the same company goes into decline the coverage often concludes that the fault lies in bad decisions taken by those in charge, or that success led them to become complacent and lose focus on the customer. 'Company performance, good or bad, creates an overall impression – a halo – that shapes how we perceive its strategy, leaders, employees, culture, and other elements,' wrote business school professor Philip Rosenzweig in his brilliant book *The Halo Effect*. Rosenzweig noted how journalists, authors and academics rush to create case studies of 'great companies' based entirely on outcomes such as stock price performance, increased revenues or profitability.

These detailed stories are packaged up and presented as templates for success that others are encouraged to follow.

Like the Good Captain, the people in charge when the success happened are given most of the credit. Yet Rosenzweig's conclusion was that most of these case studies, including some of the best-selling business books of the last 20 years, have limited universal application. Instead, they exaggerate the impact of leadership style and management practices on results, and that rather than being a template for high performance, these attribution errors have helped create a misleading picture of what a leader looks like.

'We see the result and retrospectively alter our judgement of the people in charge,' wrote Rosenzweig. 'Show me a company that delivers high performance, and I can always find something positive to say about the person in charge. Show me a company that has fallen on hard times, and I can always find some reason to explain why the leader failed.'

The mistakes made by business and political journalists and authors are exactly those sports writers use when creating the captain myth. The job of a sports journalist is to explain what is happening on the field of play and to tell the story of the event, placing an interpretation or narrative arc upon what we see. The problem is that much of what happens on a golf course is ambiguous and difficult to define. The Ryder Cup is three days of chaos in which thousands of shots are hit, some great, some terrible. The quality of the golf is subject to many variables – from the weather and course conditions to the mental state, technique and ability of the players – and the performance of the teams is relative, not absolute. Success and failure depend not only on what you do but on what the other team does.

This is obvious but ignored when seeking to credit or blame the captain and the players; a captain and his team can play well and lose, or play badly and win. At Walton Heath in 1981, Sandy Lyle had eight birdies in 16 holes and lost to Tom Kite who had ten. 'If Sandy and I had played as a foursome, we would have beaten the lights out of anyone,' said Kite.

Compare Lyle's fate to that of Sam Torrance in 1985. Torrance shot 76 in the singles and won against Andy North, who put his ball in the water twice over the closing holes. Torrance birdied the 18th to give Europe its first Cup since 1957, and the image of the popular Scot, his arms outstretched on the final green, is one of the most iconic in the event's history.

Likewise, the Bad Captain can have many of the desirable traits we associate with great leadership such as experience, vision, empathy, great communication skills, sound judgement and charisma. Yet if he loses they are rendered redundant. In 2006, USA captain Tom Lehman displayed many admirable qualities. At press briefings Lehman was humble, smart and conveyed just the right blend of emotion and humour. He went to enormous lengths to prepare his team for the match against Ian Woosnam's Europe, encouraging his players to play the K Club course ahead of the match. When they got there he focused on team building by getting them to play nine holes as a 12-ball. He nudged Tiger Woods to help break down barriers between himself and the rookies who were in awe of him. Woods took Brett Wetterich and J. J. Henry for a steak supper and picked up the tab, which he paid in cash, flourishing two newly minted 100 euro notes from his wallet when the bill arrived.

The result of all this great leadership by Tom Lehman was that his team got thrashed.

By contrast, Lehman's opposite number Ian Woosnam was branded as 'pathetic' by Thomas Bjørn, whom he'd overlooked as a wildcard pick in favour of Lee Westwood and Darren Clarke. Bjørn was upset at what he saw as Woosnam's lack of communication, claiming that if Europe won it would be despite the captain not because of him. Woosnam himself had no airs and graces when it came to the job. He admitted he took a hands-off approach to the role, joking that the only time he gave a player any clubbing advice was on the 7th hole at the K Club and that led to the Swede Robert Karlsson's ball 'ending up on a TV tower'. Woosnam had the last laugh. He won.

'On the face of it, there are no grey areas in the Ryder Cup,' says Colin Montgomerie. 'You win or you lose, the points in the red and the blue column tell the story. But it's more complex than that. I've played against several great captains who have lost. Corey Pavin was a good captain in 2010. Tom Kite was a good captain in '97 and lost to Seve. Tom Lehman was a great captain in 2006 but lost to Woosnam. There's an analogy with a football manager who watches his player miss a penalty to lose the match. Is that really my fault? Did I cause that? No. But I'll tell you what – you'll get the blame.'

Montgomerie says that luck plays an underrated role, blurring our reading of who did what. Luck is a commodity that gets in the way of a good story. Fiction writers are berated if their plot turns on a moment of coincidence, yet it plays a considerable role in our lives, and in the Ryder Cup particularly. Justin Rose's 1 per cent putt at Medinah was due to huge skill and mental strength. And it was lucky too. Yet writers and academics tend to overestimate the role played by individual skill and foresight, whilst hugely underplaying the role of good and bad fortune.

With so many variables at play, sports fans and writers seek reasons that feel more concrete and tangible: namely, the points on the board. This gets things the wrong way around, mixing up outcomes and causes. The points on the board don't explain performance, they are a result of it.

The rise of the captain also reflects how we have come to think about leadership generally, which has become a modern obsession. This is in part due to changes in the way the media treats the subject. The growth of specialist business channels such as CNBC, Bloomberg and CNN Money in the 1980s and 1990s was part of the general shift in approach aimed at making the news more entertaining. Today's business reporting borrows heavily from sports journalism. Corporations are treated as teams. There are winners and losers, and the stock price and quarterly reports allow us to keep score. This was happening before the 2008 financial crisis and accelerated in the years since. The fall of Lehman Brothers and other high profile scandals such as Enron and Worldcom revealed how little we knew about how the business world really worked.

The media's approach was to reduce complex organisations to simple stories, and the public profiles of men such as Lee Iacocca of General Motors, Steve Jobs at Apple and Larry Ellison of Oracle soared. 'The difference between God and Larry,' went the saying, 'is that God does not believe he is Larry.' In Britain, privatisation under the Thatcher government of the 1980s encouraged the creation of thousands of first-time investors, private citizens who were dealing in shares for the first time. Rather than interrogate the balance sheets of their companies, many amateur and professional investors put their trust in celebrity. Business people who were usually only seen on the news were creeping into the features pages and became personalities in their own right. This process accelerated still further through the 1990s and early noughties as technology made businesses ever more complex. The dotcom era disrupted existing business models, making it harder for even experienced stock analysts to put accurate valuations on companies. In this chaos, the celebrity CEO offered a reassuringly familiar face to what were becoming hugely diverse multidimensional organisations.

Through the course of two decades, media savvy chief executives began to take over the reins of FTSE 500 companies. They hired their own publicists and put their names to ghostwritten books in order to build their personal brands around catchy-sounding leadership philosophies. Traditional management qualities such as strategic thinking, industry knowledge, and attention to detail were no longer deemed essential. These were management issues. Company shareholders, stock analysts and customers wanted something more than mere efficiency and data from their business leaders: they wanted stardust and a human story they could understand.

Sports fans and team owners want the same thing, and worship at the altar of the supercoach. This cult is celebrated each year at the Laureus World Sports Awards, an event dubbed 'the Oscars of sport' by its organisers. A year after Medinah, Europe won the Team of the Year award from a shortlist containing some of the best and most commercially valuable franchises in sport, a list that included the Red Bull Formula 1 championship-winning team, NBA championship winners Miami Heat and Spain's all-conquering national football side, which won the 2012 European Championships to add to its 2010 FIFA World Cup, only the second national side to hold football's two pre-eminent trophies simultaneously. Each was vying to join the club of previous winners of the Laureus team award that includes FC Barcelona, England's 2003 Rugby World Cup-winning team and Manchester United's 1999 squad which won the treble of Premier League, FA Cup and UEFA Champions League. The Laureus also sees the annual coronation of the superstar coach. Men such as Sir Clive Woodward, Sir Alex Ferguson, Christian Horner, José Mourinho and Pep Guardiola have all basked in its reflective glow. And Pat Riley.

Riley is famous as the head coach of Miami Heat and as a man with one of the most impressive CVs in American sport. Riley has managed five NBA championship teams, was elected NBA coach of the year three times, and led the LA Lakers and New York Knicks before building the Heat's 2012 and 2013 championship-winning teams. Beyond his great résumé, Riley transcends the sports arena in America. His slicked back hair and Armani tailoring was the model for Gordon Gekko, the era-defining banker, as played by his good friend Michael Douglas in *Wall Street*. 'Riley was the one who nailed it. Defined a style. Set a trend,' wrote Steve Aschburner in *Sports Illustrated*. 'And showed us all that coaches could be stars in the NBA, too, beyond barking orders back in the gym or dissecting performances in the film room.'

From the early days of his managerial career Riley was lauded by the leadership industry. In 1993, he wrote a book called *The Winner Within: A Life Plan for Team Players*, and took what he had learnt on the basketball court into the boardrooms of corporate America. His book came with the endorsement of Anthony Robbins, the famous self-help evangelist, author and motivational speaker: 'Pat Riley is a true master. No one committed to success can afford to miss this opportunity to learn from the coach of the decade.'

Riley's book was followed by motivational videos. 'Using exciting footage of the LA Lakers in action, Riley shows how managers, businesses and other organisations can apply his teamwork concepts to build a unified and motivated team,' ran the blurb. Stories of Riley's motivational tactics became the stuff of American sports legend. During the Heat's 2006 championship-winning season, Riley used a large bowl that was placed in the centre of the locker room, into which the players would post small pieces of card. Thousands of the cards were made, each bearing the words '15 Strong' on one side, and a blank space for a personal message on the other. The players were encouraged to write slogans, mottos or drawings of the Larry O'Brien trophy, the prize for winning the NBA championship. By the end of the season the bowl contained 120,000 such pieces of card, each with the '15 Strong' message. 'Every game we came closer and closer and put more and more stuff in,' said one of the Heat's players Gary Payton. 'We brought a wheelbarrow in to put stuff in because he gave us a story about trusting people and pushing a wheelbarrow across a tightrope. He's a great motivator. He did what he was supposed to do. He got us to play the way we were supposed to play, and we stuck together.'

Other players described similar moments of classic Riley management techniques. He once put a large bucket of ice water in front of him and told his team, 'If you want to win a championship, you have to want it—' Stopping in mid-sentence, Riley plunged his head into the water and kept it there for several seconds, which turned into a minute, which turned into even more than a minute. His players sat dumbfounded, watching, until Riley finally pulled his head out of the water and finished his sentence, '. . . like it's your last breath.'

Riley and other charismatic supercoaches have framed the issue of leadership in a sporting context. The problem is that this is a very narrow definition. The Pat Riley model suggests that the power to influence the team is in the hands of the man at the top, casting the team in a subservient role. It positions the captain, coach or manager as the protagonist, and the team as reacting to his lead, painting the golfers as passive receivers of his wisdom, experience and motivational zeal: the captain acts and the team responds.

On the contrary, wrote Archie Brown in *The Myth of the Strong Leader*, good leadership should never be confused with the 'overmighty power of overweening individuals'. When a captain is charismatic, autocratic and eloquent we are quick to describe them as demonstrating strong leadership, where the terms 'strong' and 'good' appear interchangeable. This is a common mistake. 'The latter is not an abstract attribute but an appropriate response in a distinctive setting – in a particular time and place,' noted Brown.

Instead, leadership is closely linked to context. What is appropriate or possible in one situation may be inappropriate or unattainable in another. 'Leadership styles differ in war and peace and in a crisis as compared to calmer times.' The strong–weak dichotomy is just one of several. 'Charismatic leaders are set against mere office holders, innovators compared with bureaucrats, real leaders with managers, while transforming leaders are distinguished from transactional leaders. Great leaders with ordinary leaders, good or bad and, of course, strong and weak.'

Where the Ryder Cup captain differs from most sports coaches is that he usually only gets one go at the job. When the captain is doing it for the first and probably only time it changes the dynamic and makes him, by definition, less influential than a team coach or manager, who is there day in day out sometimes for years on end. The team coach can tinker with his philosophy through trial and error, trying out man-management techniques and strategy options without the worry that they will come to define him in quite the same way. This is an important distinction because leadership is often subtle. It is a comment here, a look there, a gentle prod followed by an arm around the shoulder. The relationships fostered under pressure are useful for later on. The Ryder Cup captain rarely has a later on. He only has the here and now.

With this constraint, the temptation is to go too big with the statements, too large in fear of the players misunderstanding or misreading the intentions. There is no record of work that adds to the gravitas of the captain's decision-making, no record of trophies or winners' medals, or manager of the month awards. The captain is famous for playing golf, not leading teams or devising strategy or making speeches, or any of the hundred and one things he is now expected to do. This insecurity can drive captains to demonstrate their leadership philosophy in a heavy-handed way; too much the autocrat perhaps, the 'my way or the highway' approach. The opposite is also bedecked with problems. Too open and democratic, and a captain leaves himself vulnerable to the post-result accusation of being weak and indecisive. 'He couldn't make a decision without consulting everyone' is a common complaint of a losing captain.

We prefer to think of team performance as being a direct consequence of the manager's actions, but if leadership was that easy we'd all be doing it. The former England cricket captain Mike Brearley put this into a sporting perspective when he wrote the influence of the captain on a team is 'continuous and elusive . . . the decision-making process is often a matter of ideas being thrown in, played with, criticised, until it is hard to say whose idea it is that the captain eventually acts on – and is judged by. In retrospect it is easier to recall the spectacular successes and defeats rather than the buzz of reflection, intuition, bluff and memory that actually makes up the job.'

Brearley's description captures perfectly how we simplify the messy nature of the leader–follower relationship. Captaincy is not 'something you have done to you', to borrow 1999 European captain Mark James's phrase, it is more like a story we choose to believe.

Chapter 5

When There's No Difference Between Them and Us

The captain has become more prominent as the differences between the two Ryder Cup teams, in reality, have reduced. Today's elite golfers have far more in common than ever before, and most of the 24 players across both teams play in a similar style, compete in the same tournaments and play and practise at the same courses. They fly together on private jets and some even live in the same luxurious gated communities in Florida. Of the 14½ points won by Europe at Medinah, ten came from residents of Florida. Justin Rose, Ian Poulter, Graeme McDowell, Rory McIlroy, Lee Westwood and Peter Hanson each lived in or around Orlando at that time. Luke Donald also has a home in Florida, although he spends most of his time in Chicago, which has been his home since attending Northwestern University as a teenager.

The match in 2012 merely confirmed what we already knew. The market for golfing talent is a global one, as it is for most other highly paid professions. To show just how little difference there is between the teams, look at some of the performance data on the 24 players who lined up at Medinah. Using statistics from the 2012 PGA Tour season, *Golf Digest* analysed the line-ups to show just how similar the players had become. This analysis compared driving distance and accuracy across both the American and European teams.

There are only minor differences between the stats of the two teams. Some are longer, some are straighter; on average the

Player, Fairways %, Avg. drive yardage

European Team, 62.66, 292.0

- Nicolas Colsaerts, 55.77, 317.3
- Luke Donald, 62.90, 274.7
- Sergio García, 61.41, 292.4
- Peter Hanson, 59.60, 297.5
- Martin Kaymer, 63.39, 289.4
- Paul Lawrie, 53.20, 290.4
- Graeme McDowell, 71.19, 285.5
- Rory McIlroy, 55.94, 310.1
- Francesco Molinari, 74.45, 277.0
- Ian Poulter, 68.43, 280.9
- Justin Rose, 64.26, 290.9
- Lee Westwood, 61.44, 298.1

U.S. team, 62.71, 293.6
- Keegan Bradley, 62.54, 302.7
- Jason Dufner, 66.37, 292.4
- Jim Furyk, 70.91, 279.9
- Dustin Johnson, 57.38, 310.2
- Zach Johnson, 68.31, 281.3
- Matt Kuchar, 63.71, 286.2
- Phil Mickelson, 55.37, 294.4
- Webb Simpson, 60.96, 288.6
- Brandt Snedeker, 60.56, 288.7
- Steve Stricker, 64.72, 285.4
- Bubba Watson, 58.67, 315.5
- Tiger Woods, 63.06, 297.4

Americans were 1.6 yards per drive longer than Europe. In terms of fairway accuracy there is only 0.05 per cent difference between the two teams.

What is clear is that there is no evidence of a distinct American or European style of play. In fact, if we were to throw the 24 players' names into a hat and divide the two teams randomly, it seems likely that a match of similar quality and closeness would occur. The reasonable conclusion we can draw is that the very best golfers in the world are very similar and becoming more so. A standard golfing technique has evolved.

The reason for this homogeneity in the world's best golfers is replicated in most sports, lessening the impact of geography and national identity, making 'them and us' more difficult to discern. The elevation of the captaincy is in part a response to this issue, adding a point of difference between the teams.

The End of Geography

When Walter Hagen led the first American team in 1927, the impact of geography on the golf swing was still apparent. The style of golf played by the American golfers was often noticeably different to that of the British players. Today, teaching methods and exposure to television have smoothed out the differences in players' swings, says Dave Pelz. 'I defy anyone who says they can tell where a player comes from by looking at their golf swing.'

For Scotland's first golfing pioneers, there was very little reward for hitting the ball in the air. They played on rough coastal links land with a ball made of duck down, or wet feathers, which hardened when dry. To counter these challenges, they developed a low, slingy 'St Andrews swing'. This more closely resembled that of a baseball hitter than the more upright golf swing as we would know it today.

By the time the game was exported to America in the late 19th century, new types of balls and clubs were developed that made it easier to hit the ball in the air. Golf technique evolved accordingly, and swings became more upright. Teaching was carried out mainly by club professionals who copied the best players of the day. The country clubs of America contained lakes and sand traps, further encouraging players to hit over them. In the era of hickory shafted clubs, players such as Hagen and his early Ryder Cup teammate Gene Sarazen controlled the whip-like torque generated by the shaft by using their hands, allowing them to hit the ball higher and further. When Hagen first went to Britain to play the Open Championship, observers noted how his technique was seemingly ill-suited to the rigours of links courses, where the Open has always been played. Hagen, like many Americans of this time, hit a high ball and found it being blown off line by the strong coastal winds. However, he was a good enough player to adapt his game accordingly and went on to win the Open Championship four times in his career.

Over the course of the Ryder Cup's history, the golf swing has evolved in response to changes in equipment, playing conditions and the increased knowledge and application of biomechanical principles. The growth of video through the 1970s allowed everyone to see how the words in the books and magazines did not always match the pictures. Opinion began to give way to measurable fact.

This was a theme developed by the writer and former England Test cricketer Ed Smith, in his book *Luck*. Smith discussed the effect of globalisation on cricket and, in particular, on batting technique, which, like the golf swing, has become homogenised. 'It is undermining our old clichés about sport and nationality,' wrote Smith. 'It has also propagated, in each sport, a dominant style of play. We are now part of a worldwide sporting community, not just a national or local one.'

Smith noted that today's Indian batsmen, for example, no longer followed the classic 'wristy Indian' stereotype. Players from the subcontinent were traditionally excellent players of spin bowling because of the type of pitches on which they learnt the game, which favoured the slower bowlers. Before cable and satellite television, the only prolonged exposure to cricket came from watching other Indian batsmen playing in their local area. This has changed. Today, Indian batsmen play a different type of game that is similar to that played by the best players in other countries. The great star of Indian cricket is M. S. Dhoni, who is famous for playing a power game, based on forceful drives and an array of back-foot shots, such as the cut and hook shots. Dhoni has taken the best parts of batsmanship from other cultures and melded it together. The cut and hook shots are what cricket fans traditionally associate with Australian batsmen, who were reared on fast bouncy pitches, which encouraged fast bowling. The batsmen's technique evolved to counter that threat. Likewise, English batsmen were confronted with a series of different problems. The slower, lower pitches and wetter conditions rewarded bowlers who were able to make the ball move sideways off the pitch. To counter this English batsmen learnt to reduce the effect of the ball's lateral movement by moving towards the ball as it bounced, playing front-foot shots such as the drive.

Like M. S. Dhoni, Justin Rose is playing a global game rather than a local one. Rose is a rare golfer who is famous beyond the bubble of the game's core support, possessing two assets that are much valued in today's sports marketplace. He has a great swing and a great story. He was the 17-year-old wunderkind who came so close to winning the Open Championship as an amateur, at Royal Birkdale in 1998. He holed out on the final green to come fourth behind that year's winner, the American player Mark O'Meara, taking the silver medal for leading amateur. The journey from the 18th green at Birkdale to the 17th tee at Medinah was anything but a straight line, however, and like the hero of all the best tales, Rose's story took a series of turns before he got to his happy ending. He turned pro the day after the '98 Open, with expectations running high in the media. The subtext to the press coverage was that Britain had found another Faldo.

Then, over the following weeks and months, the story changed as Rose missed his first 21 cuts as a pro. Week by week through the latter part of 1998 the Rose bubble slowly deflated and his name receded from the back pages. It was one of the cruellest and most extended periods of public examination faced by any sportsman in any field. He went from being that kid who nearly won the Open, to being famous for failure, a case study of what can happen when fame comes too soon. He came through the experience, supported every step of the way by Ken Rose, who combined his role as father with that of mentor and coach. Like Dhoni's global batting technique, the development of Justin Rose's swing lies in a combination of factors that include talent, hours of practice and excellent teaching from a young age. And television. Rose is of a generation of players who have grown up with satellite and cable television, with sports channels showing golf from around the world on an almost daily basis. Rather than copy the swings of the players he saw in person at a local tournament, Rose and his father Ken were able to take their pick of the best players in the world as their swing model. Why wouldn't they? As good as they are, why would you pick a swing as personal and idiosyncratic as say, the Irish Ryder Cup player Eamonn Darcy, or the American Jim Furyk, over the more aesthetically pleasing motions of a Nick Faldo or Ernie Els?

Look out at the players on the practice range at a Major championship, said Rory McIlroy in 2015 – it's very hard to tell them apart. 'Everyone hits the ball great, strikes it well. It's just the minute differences, making good decisions, deciding when to be aggressive.'

Despite this, the way we talk of today's teams reflects the past not the present.

Set-Up, Joke

At a press conference in the week of the 2014 Cup at Gleneagles, an American journalist asked European captain Paul McGinley how he had chosen to set up the course. On hearing the question, McGinley smiled as though greeting an old friend. The set-up question is a hardy perennial throughout the tenure of every home captain, and his response was delivered as though by rote. 'I haven't gone out of my way to trick things up,' said McGinley. 'I'd like to think I'm playing it very straight this week when it comes to the course set-up. I've aligned it very much with the set-up that we play on the European Tour.'

The home captain has the option to alter the course to suit his own team, and this is one of the few areas he can be seen to have a tangible impact. Broadly speaking, these decisions can be broken into three categories: the speed of the greens, the width of the fairways and the length of the rough, both along the fairway and around the green itself. 'In general we have narrower fairways in Europe than you do on the PGA Tour,' continued McGinley. 'In general we have a little bit more rough and in general the American greens are quicker and faster than we have on the European Tour.'

The media likes the set-up question because it hints at secret strategy and skulduggery. As home captain at Medinah two years previously, Davis Love used the opportunity to shape the conditions to fit what he called his 'long-hitting, freewheeling, fun-to-watch team'. Love ordered Medinah's course superintendent to lower the blades on the mowers to the extent that the intermediate (or semi) rough was reduced to 1¼ inches for ten yards either side of the fairways. This had the effect of turning Medinah's 30-yard wide fairways into a target 50 yards wide. Even when they missed that target, there was little to fear because Love had ordered that the main rough was kept at 2½ inches, allowing players to 'bomb and gouge' their way around the course.

'It's not that big a deal,' said Paul Azinger. 'Europe started doing that when America had a few really big hitters, Tiger and Phil included.'

'It was clear that Sam Torrance had cut some of the fairways off at the Belfry [in 2002],' said Azinger. 'Everyone then was driving the same length off the tee because of the way the fairways had been cut and the rough grown up. It neutralised America's strength, which was power. It was the first time I'd noticed that.'

In 1999 the American team was led by the popular Texan player Ben Crenshaw, a veteran of four Cups as a player and who made his debut in Dave Marr's 'dream team' of 1981. In contrast to Mark James's Europeans, Crenshaw's team was packed with players with previous Ryder Cup experience. There was just one rookie – David Duval – who was surrounded by Major championship winners, many of whom came into the week on top form. Part of the American captain's pre-match strategy might be best termed 'courses for horses'. As the home captain, it was Crenshaw's prerogative to set up the Brookline course in a way that gave his team the most advantage. He sought to reward his big hitters – Tiger Woods, Davis Love, Phil Mickelson and David Duval – by paring back the rough at the 300-yard mark and encouraging them to go for it off the tee, safe in the knowledge they could hack it to the green if they were wide.

The reverse of this strategy was employed in 1997 by Europe captain Seve Ballesteros when he set up the Valderrama course in Spain to try to limit the Americans' length advantage off the tee.

Mark James was one of Ballesteros's non-playing assistant captains and recalled a meeting with the Spaniard where they discussed other ways of using the course to their team's advantage. 'I want you to watch the Americans,' said Ballesteros to James, suggesting he go on a reconnaissance mission during the practice rounds. 'What, spy on them?' said James, startled by the idea of following the American captain Tom Kite around the course.

Seve nodded his head, and in particular wanted to know how they were playing the long 17th hole. He wanted to know whether they could reach the long par-5 17th green in two shots, rather than the regulation three. This would give Tom Kite's team a distinct advantage. By hitting a longer tee shot down the fairway, players such as Woods and Mickelson were able to fly their second shot onto the green and set up a putt for an eagle three, or two under the hole's par of five shots. Europe's shorter hitters would need three shots to reach the green, which was protected at the front by a small lake. Ballesteros was worried that the hole offered greater birdie opportunities for the visitors as many of the matches would be reaching a conclusion.

When he saw James loitering around behind the ropes, Tom Kite asked what the Englishman thought he was doing. 'It's OK,' said James, 'Seve has sent me to spy on you.' Kite assumed James was joking and laughed it off. The story reveals the perceived differences between the teams at this point. 'The Americans generally hit higher with less spin whereas our boys went in lower with more action on the ball,' wrote James in his account of the Brookline match, *Into the Bear Pit*. 'Their players were actually holding it [the 17th green] better, so we sat for the best part of an hour debating the issue: should we soak it so everybody could hold it, or shave it so nobody could. We rolled balls off the front right of the green to see if they would trickle into the water.' Ballesteros instructed the greenkeeper to grow the grass across the middle of the fairway. This was to discourage America's longer hitters from trying to reach the par 5 in two shots, rather than the regulation three. It caused quite a bit of consternation within his own team too. Colin Montgomerie recalls playing the hole in practice at that 1997 Cup: 'I'll never forget the 17th hole. There was myself, there was Langer, Faldo and Woosnam, all Major champions. That was my fourth Ryder Cup, so I had a bit of experience too, and we played the 17th hole in practice and we played it quite badly, the four of us. We made a bit of a mess of it. We went on to the 18th hole, finished the round, and Seve came over and he said, "No, no, I want you to all go back to the 17th hole and play properly." And I looked at Faldo and he looked at me and Woosnam, and Langer. It was like, "What has he just told us to do?" These guys, including myself, I was the number two in world at the time. It was like schoolboy stuff, but he was dead right and he was in charge and we respected him for that. Sometimes the hardest decisions are the ones for which you gain the most respect from the team.'

Azinger was another captain who attempted to manipulate conditions in his own team's favour. In 2008 he made a point of bonding with the course superintendent at Valhalla: 'If I've got J. B. Holmes who hits it 300 yards in the air and hits it sideways, why would I want rough past 300 yards? It was just logical. My team had great ball strikers and great iron players but weren't necessarily real accurate off the tee, so I didn't feel the need to have a lot of big rough. I wanted the rough grown around the greens because America is used to that compared to Europe, where they are more familiar with a mown area.'

There's general agreement that such tactics are more about psychology than seeking any real advantage. 'We all play in America now so it doesn't matter,' said Azinger, whose views were echoed by Paul McGinley at Gleneagles: 'There was a time when we were straighter and shorter and they were longer and a little bit wider, but that's not the case any more. It's one of the reasons why it wasn't a case of me trying to outsmart myself. I wanted to make sure our players were going to be comfortable, and if the Americans are comfortable, too, so be it.'

This poses a problem for an event like the Ryder Cup that makes great play of the cultural, historical and playing differences between the two teams. Transposed to the Ryder Cup, the homogeneity of today's players means fans, the media and the players themselves must seek ways of differentiating between the two teams. To do this we rely on the captain to tell us a story.

A Team With a Story Attached

In 2010 two business writers, Joshua Glenn and Rob Walker, carried out an experiment. They had noticed that many of the products we buy on a day-to-day basis were becoming hard to tell apart. Globalisation and production techniques had narrowed the gap in quality between different brands, from mobile phones to cars to burgers. This has created a basic business problem: why do we buy one product over another, when we perceive both to be, at their core, the same?

The answer to this question is that we respond to the stories about the product created by the advertising industry. A popular working definition of 'a brand' is a product with a story attached. Brand stories are sometimes 'authentic' but often completely made up. Anyone in the market for an Aston Martin sports car will know that it is 'the car James Bond drives', whereas whiskey drinkers are sometimes reminded that Frank Sinatra was reportedly buried with a bottle of Jack Daniel's in his coffin. The Swedish car maker Saab established its reputation for quirky, eccentric design in the 1960s and 1970s, making them popular with culturally discerning car buyers, a story that was harder to sustain once the cars themselves were built by the American conglomerate General Motors, which bought Saab in 2000.

Glenn and Walker set about trying to prove how everyday products rose in value when a story was created for them. The results were staggering, and in some ways help explain what we see when we watch the modern Ryder Cup and other professional sports events.

The two men bought a number of cheap throwaway objects from charity shops and car boot sales for free or for very small amounts of money. They then invited authors to write a fictional story about the objects, after which they listed both the product and the story for sale on eBay. The effect was that bland, undifferentiated products were given a new lease of life. A used and discarded yo-yo that had cost 25 cents at a boot sale was sold on eBay for $41, a mark-up of 16,400 per cent. The only difference between the 25-cent yo-yo and its more expensive version was the fictional backstory written by the author Mark Sarvas. This involved a young garage mechanic who learnt to use the yo-yo to impress a girl. In the imagination of the buyer, the yo-yo was transformed from a basic, undifferentiated item into something that engaged them on an emotional level. For the first 100 items bought, 'storied' and resold on eBay, the average object purchase price was $1.29. The average resale price after a story was added was $36.12, making an average increase in value of 2,800 per cent. Glenn and Walker's experiment showed how we rely on brand stories to separate undifferentiated goods.

The analogy with sport is not a perfect one by any means. Sports fans don't choose their team in the same way as they do a mobile phone. The decision is less rational, often coming down to where we were born or which team talked to us at influential moments in our lives. However, the way we talk and feel about sports teams has parallels with Glenn and Walker's work. Just as the ad men plunder the past to tell brand stories, so coaches, managers and captains use a carefully selected version of history to create team myths that help make sense of the present. The job of a coach is to create a sense of shared values and to unite the group in pursuing common goals. To do this they must answer the questions 'Who are we?' and 'Where are we going?'

The answers to these questions lie in the past, and the Good Captain has become adept at ransacking history to link their current group of players to illustrious predecessors.

Chapter 6

The Gatsby Analogy

The first two captains played against each other on the first day of the inaugural Ryder Cup in 1927. Walter Hagen and his playing partner Johnny Golden were pitched against British captain Ted Ray and Fred Robson. The simple facts of the 1927 Ryder Cup were that America beat Great Britain convincingly by 9 ½ to 2 ½, and in many ways the exploits of players such as Walter Hagen and Ted Ray bear little relevance to today's Ryder Cup. It was another time and place, and the matches have evolved over the best part of a century to become almost unrecognisable. Yet the way we talk about today's event – how we frame our descriptions of the two teams, and even some of the decisions made by present day captains – has its genesis in those early matches.

The notes of G. A. Philpot, the manager of the 1927 British team, offer an insight into the divide between the two teams. Philpot wrote about being greeted by 'a great crowd that had assembled to give us welcome' at Manhattan docks, followed by cocktails at the Westchester Country Club, dinner and a vaudeville show.

The next day, Hagen organised for the visitors to watch their first ever baseball match at Yankee Stadium, where Babe Ruth led the home team to a surprise defeat to the visiting Washington Senators. After the match Ruth invited the British pros to share a night on the town with him and Hagen in Manhattan. It may tell us something about the difference between the two teams that the prospect of a night out in the city that never sleeps with two of its most famous inhabitants was politely declined. The British team went back to their hotel to prepare to play golf. They should have taken Babe's offer: after the excesses of the welcome party, the match at Worcester was something of an anti-climax, with the British putting exposed on the quicker, expensively manicured greens.

The format of the first match was different to the one we are familiar with today. The matches were played over two days rather than three. The first day consisted of four 36-hole foursome matches, while the second and final day was made up of eight singles games, again over 36 holes.

The British pair of Ray and Robson had the better of the morning's play and were three up when the teams broke for lunch. It was an up and down type of game. Hagen and Golden won three of the first five holes in the afternoon but then lost the next three. Their inconsistency was summed up at the par-3 eighth hole. After Johnny Golden left his tee shot in the sand, Hagen hit it out of bounds.

By contrast, the British pair was ham and egging relatively well, with Robson's accurate iron play setting up Ray for birdie opportunities. 'At the ninth Robson played a spectacular slice round some trees to within ten feet of the hole,' wrote a reporter from *The Times* of London.

Ray's putter let him down, however, and he squandered a number of chances to capitalise. The turning point came midway through the afternoon round, when the Americans combined to win four holes in a row, from the 12th to the 15th, to take a one-shot lead. Hagen holed a three-foot birdie putt on the 16th to go two up and the teams halved the 17th. Hagen and Golden had run out 2 and 1 winners, shaking hands with the British pair on the 17th green. This would be the story for the next 30 years, as Britain won just once between 1927 and 1957.

The Intoxicating Fake

Walter Hagen is a defining figure in Ryder Cup history. He was captain of the American team for the first six matches, and more than any other person he came to represent a version of America that remained in place, and in the minds of foreign golfers, for more than 50 years. Although a truly great player, his enduring image had little to do with how he played golf.

'He has refashioned himself into a colourful personage, like a grand opera tenor, or movie top liner,' was how the *New York Times* described Hagen in 1927. 'He seldom moves without three trunks of clothes. His valet is in constant attendance. He drives only the flashiest cars. He wears lemon yellow gloves and spats upon occasion. Hagen has elevated a lowly profession to the heights of a lucrative and decorative art. He has crowned it with dignity, and enriched it with elegance.'

Alistair Cooke, the BBC's man in America for most of the 20th century, wrote a beautiful obituary of Hagen in 1969. Cooke was a great journalist and a keen golfer, and he was a friend and fan of Hagen's. 'Throughout the twenties, few Englishmen knew even what an American sounded like,' wrote Cooke. 'He was a species of the exotic. Most of us in those days kept a file at the back of our minds of what we took to be standard American types, compiled naturally from the silent movies.' Into this vacuum walked Hagen, 'with the head of a seal, the sleepy eyes, the peacock sweaters and the co-respondent's shoes, and his much-publicised love of the high life.' He looked, wrote Cooke, like the lounge lizard all nice girls were warned about. 'The stories were meant to make us chuckle, but in the beginning the chuckles were punctuated by pained cries from the Old Guard whom the Lord sent Hagen to mock.'

It's impossible to read the life of Walter Hagen without some reference to F. Scott Fitzgerald's great literary creation, Jay Gatsby. *The Great Gatsby* was a story of glittering excess, of a gilded society intoxicated by wealth, dancing its way into the Great Depression. It's a novel about the allure, corruption and carelessness of wealth, personified by Gatsby 'the intoxicating fake, the impossibly famous nobody, adored and envied by all but known to none, who yet has something gorgeous about him, some heightened sensitivity to the promises of life'. To fall in love with Gatsby is to fall in love with America, wrote Ben Macintyre. 'Gatsby is America, dazzling, self-invented, striving and flawed, now, then and always.'

Golf's history books are littered with the achievements of the great players, whose careers were defined in terms of Major victories and money won. Hagen is different. He is one of a very few golfers who became famous beyond the clubhouses and fairways.

'When other great players will be remembered only by the photographs of their swing and the tournament statistics,' wrote

Alistair Cooke, 'Walter Hagen will be immortal for certain other records that recall not so much his prowess as his brash charm and his delight in the game: the first man to give his caddie all his prize money; the first, and perhaps the only, first-class player who had the gall to have the flag removed for a long-iron approach from about 170 yards; the only professional who ever jerked a putt out of bounds; and always the only golfer who honestly and always forgot the last bad hole. For these things and also for the remark, practically a capsule philosophy, that does not dim by endless repetition and which would have made the perfect epitaph for his gravestone: "take the time to smell the flowers".'

The Man Who Created Sir Walter

The stories about Walter Hagen are so good that it's hard to get beyond the cartoonish caricature to the real man who was so instrumental in creating the professional golf tour in America, and in establishing the Ryder Cup itself. And just as Jay Gatsby was the creation of F. Scott Fitzgerald, the story of Walter Hagen was, in part at least, a work of fiction, written by a professional storyteller.

After he won the US Open for the second time, in 1919, Hagen hired a 32-year-old golf journalist called Bob Harlow to handle his business and PR affairs. Pre-Harlow, Walter Hagen was largely indistinguishable from other golf professionals of the day. He was a family man who married his teenage sweetheart in the summer of 1916, rarely if ever drank alcohol and dressed in the sober palette typical of the working golf pro. By the time the Ryder Cup began in 1927, however, Hagen was not just a golfer, he was 'Sir Walter'.

Hagen recognised the debt he owed Harlow in building his brand. 'He took over that position just prior to my embarking for the second attempt to win the British Open and he was my big noise for some ten years,' wrote Hagen later.

Harlow was the son of a congregational minister and came from a middle-class family in Newburyport, Massachusetts. He was far more than just a PR man, though: he became one of the most significant figures in the development of the American professional game. After he left Hagen's employ he went on to work for the PGA of America, using the network of golf exhibitions he had built for Hagen as the basis of what we now know as the PGA Tour. Later, Harlow would create *Golf World* magazine, and his contribution was given official recognition when he was inducted into golf's Hall of Fame. Harlow's role has parallels to that played two generations later by Mark McCormack, who helped create the Arnold Palmer brand in the 1960s. Like McCormack, Harlow was a master in the manipulation of sporting celebrity for commercial gain, turning Hagen from a very good golfer into one of the stars of American sport's first 'golden age'.

He was the man best equipped to sell the tour to America Inc., and was adept at working the levers of commerce that remain in place today. Harlow would convince local business leaders and chambers of commerce to sponsor events in the hope of economic and reputational benefit, in the form of tourism and increased business for local services. The course would get a higher profile and could up its rates.

Harlow often used analogies with the film industry: 'Golfers cannot do their best playing to empty fairways any better than actors can give a fine performance to empty chairs. You, the pros, are definitely in the show business, buy a copy of the theatrical magazine *Variety*, and absorb some of the atmosphere to be found in the pages of this journal of masks and wiggers.'

The importance of Harlow runs further than his ability to spin stories. He and Hagen were culturally different to the people at the PGA of America, who ran the game. Harlow brought the spirit of the entrepreneur to golf, and represented a new breed who saw golf as an entertainment product, a philosophy that rubbed against the world view of the PGA, who saw themselves as a trade union of the club pros.

This fault line remains visible today. The PGA of America, which owns and runs the Ryder Cup, represents golf professionals across the country at local clubs. In 1968, the PGA Tour was established to take ownership, marketing and commercialisation of the tournament schedule of the elite players. It's the PGA Tour, under the leadership of Deane Beman and more recently Tim Finchem that is the basis of the top players' incomes and extravagant lifestyles. When Team USA loses the Ryder Cup the players' allegiances to the PGA of America are sometimes questioned: why is it they seem to perform better in the PGA Tour's own biennial team competition, the Presidents Cup, than at the Ryder Cup?

While Bob Harlow's storytelling skill may have been the basis of Walter Hagen's captain myth, the message needed to be amplified beyond the golfing world. This was achieved through a vibrant new medium that changed how news was delivered to America, the tabloid newspaper.

If you had a racy tale to tell, or desire to scandalise and shock, America in 1927 was the perfect place to do it. The rise of the tabloids prompted a huge hike in the market for news. In the 1920s newspaper sales rose by a fifth to 36 million copies a day, or

1.4 newspapers for every household. New York City alone had 12 daily papers and all other cities had at least two or three. Just as significantly for the Hagen story, the tabloids changed how news was defined, shifting the agenda towards crime stories, sport and entertainment gossip. In his book, *One Summer, America, 1927,* Bill Bryson described the invention and rise of the tabloid newspaper as a new phenomenon 'not just in the format, but also in the kind of attitude'. A study in 1927 showed that tabloids devoted between a quarter and a third of their space to crime reports, up to ten times more than so-called serious newspapers did. Sport got a far bigger billing too, and as a result a tranche of sportsmen became celebrities: Babe Ruth, Johnny Weissmuller and Hagen moved from the back to the front pages, and were as likely to be photographed in tuxedos as sports kit.

With Harlow at the controls, stories about Hagen's golfing prowess were pushed to the margins in favour of two of tabloid journalism's more popular themes: money and sex.

'The party lasted all night . . . Champagne, pretty girls, jokes and laughter . . . no sleep,' wrote Hagen (or Harlow) of the night before the player's victory at the US Open at Brae Burn, when he was said to have been living it up with Al Jolson. The singer was in Boston for a ten-week run of *Sinbad* at the city's opera house.

And his friendship with Babe Ruth only helped cement Hagen's image as a hellraiser. 'What Babe wanted was a chicken dinner and daughter combination, and it worked out that way more often than you would think,' said Marshall Hunt, sports editor of the *New York Daily News.* Another leading sportswriter of the time, Fred Lieb, recalled watching Ruth being pursued through a train as it sped through Louisiana. He was chased by a woman armed with a knife, the wife of a local politician, and escaped by jumping off the train as it drew to a halt at a station, then jumping back onto the next carriage, losing the woman in the process. The partying was part of the legend. 'Any woman who doesn't want to fuck can leave now,' shouted Ruth at an after-game party, standing on a chair in his hotel suite in Detroit.

Ruth's earnings were astronomical, and Hagen's were not far behind. Figures for Hagen's annual income at this time are unreliable, varying widely between $70,000 up to $250,000 per year. By comparison, 60 per cent of American families had an income of less than $2,000 a year. Whatever the number, it is the breakdown of Hagen's income that is more revealing, giving us an insight into the life of a golf professional around the time of the Ryder Cup's creation.

Unlike Ruth, who was paid a salary by his team owners, Hagen, like all pro golfers, was a freelancer and relied on Bob Harlow's genius for marketing. 'Hagen averages over $15,000 a year in prize money, $45,000 a year from exhibition matches and his annual salary as the golf expert of the Pasadena Golf and Country Club is $30,000,' wrote Bill Cunningham, a leading sports writer of the time. Like Tiger Woods today, prize money was a relatively minor part of the pay package. And like Woods's colonisation of China and the Far East, Hagen's money-making was often dressed up as golfing outreach work, positioning him as a missionary preaching the golfing gospel.

Hagen and Harlow's pioneering zeal helped raise the status of golf professionals. Years later, Arnold Palmer, himself the son of a club pro, recognised the debt he and his fellow golfers owed to Hagen. A year before Hagen died of throat cancer in 1969, a dinner was held in his honour. Palmer, at that point still the biggest name in the sport, flew himself through some awful weather to Traverse City, Michigan to make the toast. Palmer raised a glass to the guest of honour, who by then had been rendered silent following the removal of his larynx. 'If it were not for you, Walter,' he said, 'this dinner would be downstairs in the pro shop and not in the ballroom.'

Walter Hagen's captain myth casts America and, by extension, Team USA as 'the greatest country in the world'. In *One Summer* Bill Bryson suggested that 1927 marked the moment that Americans began to view their role in the world differently: 'If you just think about the kind of American attitude in World War I, and the kind of American attitude in World War II – in World War I we were allies and participants, latecomers but we participated. World War II, we ran the show, you know? And the thing that happened in 1927 was that America was becoming the top nation on Earth and knew it. And that was a real psychological difference between before that period and after that period. Within a decade of 1927, America was not just the most economically powerful nation on Earth but it knew it and expected to be the global leader in almost every area.'

By the 1950s this shift in attitude had become embedded in the national psyche, captured by Stephen Kinzer's definition of American exceptionalism as 'the view that the United States has a right to impose its will because it knows more, sees farther, and lives on a higher moral plane than other nations . . . was to them not a platitude, but the organising principle of daily life and global politics.'

The teams that lined up for the first matches in 1927 reflected golf's enhanced social status in America, compared to the game's humble beginnings in Britain. 'What was there [in the UK] a game of the people, played on otherwise worthless links land, became here a game for gentlemen, played at private country clubs,' wrote John Updike. 'Primordial golf was a rough and ready game, wherein nothing but a club touched the ball between tee and holing out; you took the terrain and your luck as they came. But in the New World, the ideal of human perfectibility favoured medal play over matchplay, and precise and faithful scorekeeping encouraged ever more impeccable golf course conditions.'

Ryder Cup venues reflect this 'ideal of human perfectibility'. Country clubs such as Medinah, Brookline and Oak Hill were built in the early part of the 20th century to accommodate the country's new leisure classes. John Strawn captured their broader meaning in *Golf, The Greatest Game*, a book published in 1994 to celebrate the USGA's centenary: 'The USGA was an instrument in borrowing the great Scottish pastime and making it America's own. Henry James, an *émigré* to the Old World, regarded the country club as America's only contribution to civilisation. The country club meant power, and status, and finally it meant golf.'

The flipside of American exceptionalism is it turns any opponent into the underdog, a position that is more comfortable than it sounds. The role of the underdog has been exploited by every European captain since Tony Jacklin's cashmere revolution in the 1980s.

Chapter 7

Status Anxiety

There is a downside to being the greatest nation on earth. There's a lot to lose for one thing.

'Giants are not what we think they are,' wrote Malcolm Gladwell in *David and Goliath*. 'The same qualities that appear to give them strength are often the sources of great weakness.'

The Ryder Cup is a case study in Gladwell's statement. The sheer might of America carries with it assumptions of superiority, and these appear to weigh heavily on its golfers every two years.

Bob Rotella is golf's leading psychologist, who has worked with players from both teams over many years. 'I do think there is something in young kids growing up in Europe wanting to beat America at something,' he says. 'It means a lot more to people there than it does over here. I don't find kids growing up in America having their dream to beat Europe in the Ryder Cup. It means more to European players coming up.'

The psychology of underdog puts you in what Rotella describes as an 'only can win situation': 'If you win it's fantastic, it's a huge surprise and you're celebrated for it. If you're supposed to win and you win it's no big deal, but if you lose you're ripped to shreds. You can go back a long way into the history of sports, and coaches have always gone to the media with the underdog story, to take the pressure off. They may not be saying the same thing in the locker room, which tells you that at some level coaches, athletes and players are concerned about what the public thinks and what they feel about them. Look at the US ice hockey team that won the gold medal (the so-called 'Miracle on Ice' in 1980 at the Lake Placid Winter Olympics when an amateur American team beat the might of the Soviet Union's national team), they were celebrated because it went against expectations. Look at Ben Hogan after the car accident – it was the perfect situation. You have a really bad car accident, the doctor reads you the last rites. Hogan recovers, and just to play golf is an unbelievable achievement. To win is incredible. If he loses, the story is that he's lucky to be alive.'

The American players, says Rotella, would love to have the underdog tag in the Ryder Cup, and they would be more than willing to play the role, but the media and their own self-importance hasn't allowed them to. Perhaps, he said, they should learn from the career of Tiger Woods: 'One of the most amazing things about Tiger's career has been that from the age of 15 he was expected to win, he has made himself the guy who was supposed to win'. During Woods's long period as the best player in the world, says Rotella, the player seemed able to 'go and play his game without putting ridiculous pressure on himself in a negative way. I can't think of another player on the American tour that has that reputation or those expectations going into a tournament. Even Phil Mickelson, when he won the Open Championship in 2013, the story was, "Wow, it's incredible, Phil finally learnt how to win in Britain." If Tiger had won it, the story would have been, "Well, it's about time. He hasn't won one in five years."'

In 2008, Paul Azinger made a concerted effort to portray America as underdogs, even though they were playing at home. 'It will be unique to be in America on our home soil as underdogs but clearly the European team is strong,' Azinger said in the build-up. 'I think it's one of the strongest teams I've ever seen them bring across here. We will be an underdog. We are missing Tiger Woods, the greatest player on earth and arguably the greatest player ever. That's a big blow to us.'

Azinger won. The betting market around the Ryder Cup tells its own story. In the 14 matches between 1985 and 2012 the odds-on favourites have been turned over ten times. And on three of the four occasions when the favourites did prevail, there was only a point in it. A punter betting £100 on the underdogs in the ten Ryder Cups running up to 2012 would have netted a profit of £762.50, based on the prices quoted on the first morning of the match.

Little surprise then that the Europeans like to maintain their underdog status, despite winning far more than they lose. When PGA of America's Ted Bishop appointed Tom Watson for 2014, he rang his man's opposite number, Paul McGinley. 'I called Paul to congratulate him and he told me how much an idol Tom had been for him,' said Bishop. 'I have a tremendous amount of respect for Paul. I also came off the phone thinking he's as sly as a fox too. He's cast himself in the role of the underdog and that's clever.'

For Europe, it is a position that comes embedded into their origin myth.

Tony Jacklin's Underdog Story

Walter Hagen's generation of pioneering professionals had left the stage by 1957, to be replaced by a new group that included Sam Snead, Ben Hogan, Cary Middlecoff and Julius Boros. Unfortunately for America, none of these turned up to Lindrick, an inland course just outside Sheffield in the north of England. Snead and Hogan declined the invitation to make the trip and Middlecoff and Boros weren't picked after they had refused to play in that year's PGA Championship, the last Major of the year that is owned by the PGA of America, which also administers the Ryder Cup.

These absences encouraged a rare sense of optimism among the home crowd, particularly following on from the spirited performances of Great Britain and Ireland over the past two Cups. The previous events in 1953 and 1955 had seen America win by just one and four points respectively.

Walking the fairways at Lindrick was a 13-year-old schoolboy who had travelled with his golf-mad father, from their family home in Scunthorpe, just over 40 miles away. The young Tony Jacklin watched as the Great Britain team led by Dai Rees, and featuring Max Faulkner and Peter Alliss, beat Jackie Burke's side, the first time the Americans had lost since 1933. 'I was beside myself with excitement and was bouncing off the walls for days beforehand. At that point in my life I'd had no real "live" contact with a golf pro of any sort,' wrote Jacklin later. 'I always hoped the British Tour would come Lincolnshire's way so that I could see some actual players competing for a living. But it wasn't until the 1957 Ryder Cup that I had the chance to watch great players close up.' Dow Finsterwald and Tommy Bolt were 'just names in my head until that point, names I'd read in the papers,' wrote Jacklin. 'At Lindrick they became flesh and blood. I was enthralled. I watched them perform, walked close along with them, and began to fantasise that one day it was going to be me walking on the other side of the ropes.'

There are parallels between Tony Jacklin and Walter Hagen. Both rose from comparatively humble backgrounds to the very top of the game, winning the US and British Open Championships in their early twenties and becoming the most famous and best-paid golfers their country had ever produced.

Where Hagen was hanging out in New York jazz clubs and parties with the beautiful people, swapping one-liners and Martinis with Al Jolson, Babe Ruth and Johnny Weissmuller, Tony Jacklin was golf's contribution to a different period of social change, 1960s Britain. Jacklin wore outrageous lilac trousers, was friends with film stars such as Sean Connery, that era's James Bond, he had his hair cut by Vidal Sassoon and, like Hagen, had a fondness for Rolls-Royce cars. Dan Jenkins, the American golf writer, famously called Arnold Palmer 'the golfing Beatle', and for a period in the late sixties and early seventies, Jenkins' line could just as easily have been applied to Jacklin.

Again, like Hagen, Jacklin's career was a series of firsts. He was the first British player to win on the PGA Tour – the 1968 Greater Jacksonville Open – and the first to hold the British and US Open Championships concurrently, through 1969 and 1970, a feat not achieved since Ben Hogan in 1953. Jacklin was also the first player to hit a hole in one on television, and the first to have a rose named after him. He won 28 events and was one of the very small group of golfers who were famous beyond the game's own constituency of fans. He was awarded an OBE in 1970 following his US Open win at Hazeltine.

It's a CV that most pros would envy, yet Jacklin preferred to position himself as David against whatever Goliath he could find. In his autobiographies and in interviews, he defined his own life as a series of battles: with his putter, the English tabloid papers, the British taxman, the administrators of the European Tour, the commercial might of Mark McCormack's IMG or the small-minded good ol' boys he encountered on the PGA Tour in the 1960s and early 1970s. Status anxiety is the central theme in Jacklin's life story. Having left school at 15 to work in the local steel factory as an apprentice fitter, he turned pro aged 18, playing full-time on the British Tour a year later.

'We lived in such a tiny house, such close quarters,' wrote Jacklin of his childhood. 'And it wasn't just us, of course, for a whole class of post-war Britons this was simply the way it was. Terraced housing. Two up two down. A poxy little kitchen the size of a modern walk-in wardrobe. I was always cold in the house. If Dad was working the night shift, though, he'd put a fire on in the hearth when he got home about half-past six in the morning, so that when I got up to do my paper round the front room would be all warm. Dad would be fast asleep in his chair.' From a distance of more than half a century, it's easy to underestimate the gulf in lifestyles that existed between post-war Europe and America.

The Circus of Lights

The writer Albert Camus recalled his first trip to New York after the war, standing in Times Square surrounded by advertising billboards: 'I am literally stupefied by the circus of lights. I am just coming out of five years of night, and this orgy of violent lights gives me for the first time the impression of a new continent. An enormous, 50-foot high Camel billboard: a GI with his mouth wide open blows enormous puffs of real smoke.'

Jacklin's recollections of that time take Camus's description and gives it a golfing twist. 'Britain was still trying to find its sea legs after the war,' he said, talking about American players of the time. 'They were from a different world, there was a halo around them. We didn't have television, we read magazines and followed their progress from afar. There was no European Tour, it was just Britain and Ireland, in the pissing rain and gales. They had Las Vegas and Palm Springs and sunshine and flash cars.' America was the world of Frank Sinatra and Bob Hope, Marlboro cigarettes and money, a topic that Jacklin had always found 'complicated'. He recalled going to a country club for the first time and seeing American pros order a sandwich and a Coke in the locker room, then put down a large note to pay for it, sometimes leaving the room without bothering to take the drink or pick up their change: 'I was always flabbergasted by this, even when I was holding a couple of Open trophies and making a significant annual income. No doubt it jarred with my upbringing, and from the start I had an insecurity about money, about having enough, making enough, wanting more, feeling guilty about wanting more, about decisions designed to produce more, but which – made in relative haste – perhaps did the opposite. That anxious search for security was never far from my mind.'

Jacklin wasn't alone in feeling the poor relation. Peter Alliss recalled the post-war period wistfully when accepting entry into golf's Hall of Fame in 2012: 'We had funny rules and regulations. You couldn't take your wife. You [the Americans] came over with your team in the days when they came by sea, and the wives were all wearing beautiful clothes and fur coats, when fur coats were acceptable, and they were all elegant and coiffured with beautiful fingernails – ours had a cardigan on and flat shoes and three kids trailing in the background with snotty noses, and so it looked very different. You overwhelmed us with your equipment. It all looked better than ours. We were really second-rate citizens, or were made to feel that way through no fault of yours. But that was just the culture of the time.'

The Throat of the Goat

The very best cashmere is found in the downy undercoat of fine neck hair that keeps Mongolian goats warm in winter. To get at it, you have to be patient. The goats moult each spring, shedding their outer fleece of thick long hairs – the cheaper stuff – to expose the soft bounty beneath. Each animal produces three or four ounces of the luxe version, enough for between a third and a half of an average men's-size golf sweater; a sheep's wool can make up to four sweaters, which helps explain the price difference.

In the hands of Tony Jacklin, the use of cashmere went way beyond its famed qualities of warmth and velvety touch. It was a central plank of his leadership story, which has been passed down generation after generation, forming Team Europe's founding parable. To make his status story stick in the minds of his followers, Jacklin had to show why change was needed, and he has a tendency to lay it on a bit thick. The way Jacklin tells it, life as a British professional golfer in the 1970s was a version of the gulag. 'I was embarrassed,' said Jacklin. 'I remember going to the matches in '71 and Eric Brown was captain again, and nobody knew Eric Brown in America but they all knew me because I was playing full time on the American Tour and had just won the US Open. So the media guys all came around me and I said, "That's the captain over there." And they said, "Well, we don't want to talk to him we want to talk to you." The bus from the airport was full, and this bloke arrived in a Rolls-Royce. He'd seen that I had a Rolls-Royce back in England and he'd come to give me a lift. It was standing room only on the bus so I said to John Bywaters [the team secretary], "Can I go with him?" and he said, "Yeah, why not?" So this bloke drove me to the hotel. Eric was pissed off that I'd got all this attention at the airport. When we got to the hotel he came over and said, "I don't want you riding in Rolls-Royces with the rest of us riding in buses."'

Jacklin's status-based captain myth has been amplified many times by various team members down the years. Nick Faldo wrote in his autobiography, *Life Swings*, 'Given how competitive the Ryder Cup has become since 1985, it is curious to reflect that before then, we went into the contest thinking we had no chance whatsoever; we knew we were going to lose from the moment the US team was announced. We were not really a team; we were not organised. Brian Huggett [the 1977 Great Britain and Ireland captain] kept everything close to his chest in terms of his pairings. We never knew with whom we would be playing until the last moment. The whole thing was an amateurish adventure. You arrived at Royal Lytham, were handed your sweater, which was either too small or too big but never ever the right size, ordered into line to have your official team picture taken, then you teed off.'

Seve Ballesteros agreed with Faldo's memory of those days. He told the writer Robert Green that the Americans 'thought we were like the third world of golf. We were always on the losing side before we started. And that was the beginning of where the challenge and motivation came from.'

'He [Jacklin] brought the belief that we could beat the Americans,' said José María Olazábal. 'It was the first Ryder Cup for me, in 1987. We flew on Concorde, we got high-quality clothing, he made us believe we were special. And all of a sudden we were standing and looking at the Americans, saying, "Hey, we look as good as you do . . ." I think up to then, we were, let's say, like the poor cousin, as compared to the Americans. But he brought out that quality in us – here we are, well dressed, cashmere sweaters, looking really good. We looked at the Americans like the first-class guys, well dressed, looking good, blond hair . . . yeah, it was a big difference in those days.'

'I knew, you see, how it was in the States. I'd seen how organised it was over there, so I always felt that we were treated like second-class citizens,' said Jacklin. 'Self-esteem is so meaningful. How can you compete on the same level if you are treated badly – we were flying in the back of the bus, not knowing who was paying for the bloody dry cleaning, not being able to take caddies with us – everything was about what we couldn't do. The Americans came across on Concorde so I wanted us to go on Concorde. I wanted the best clothes – we had always just worn anything they would give us: crap. Plastic Stylo shoes – my shoe sole came off in one match at Laurel Valley. Utter crap. It summed us up.'

Jacklin's cashmere story sees status as the major factor in Europe's renaissance in the 1980s. By removing the perceived lifestyle imbalance between America's golfers and those of Europe, Jacklin pumped up his team, who then went on to play better golf, laying the foundation for a generation of success.

But this is a flawed interpretation for several reasons, not least part of our need for simple explanations. It ignores the presence in Europe's team room of some very high-quality golfers who were winning Major championships during this period without the need of Jacklin's leadership skills. Attributing the rise of European golf to Jacklin's clothing decisions undermines the sheer brilliance of Ballesteros, Faldo, et al., and the relative decline in quality of America's best players.

There's another reason for questioning Jacklin's cashmere and Concorde myth, which is that a rise in status, real or perceived, does not in itself motivate anyone to try harder – a point that was established as far back as the 1950s. Students of motivation theory would recognise Jacklin's use of cashmere and Concorde as 'a hygiene factor', the central pillar of the work of Frederick Herzberg and Abraham Maslow. These two clinical psychologists led a step change in the way the leadership industry thought about the workplace. In the black and white days of the 1920s, when Walter Hagen and Ted Ray were teeing it up in Worcester, Massachusetts, the world's leading business thinkers were men such as Frederick W. Taylor and Max Weber. They were seeking management solutions to the problems of mass production. Factories were created to make cars and fridges and radios to feed a new breed of consumer, who wanted good, cheap products. To manage the workflow on the factory floor, Weber and Taylor created bureaucracy, the management system which remains the abiding organisational principle most of us live with today. It was the formula developed that underpinned mass production, and it has endured for so long because it worked, albeit at a huge cost in terms of human misery for the people who worked in their factories.

By the mid-fifties, as the great American triumvirate of Ben Hogan, Sam Snead and Byron Nelson dominated the game of golf, the received wisdom as to how to treat people at work had altered. Taylor's ideas were seen as backward, brutal and simplistic. People, it turns out, are not machines. They have feelings and emotions, most of which are not left at the factory gate or at the door of the office. Herzberg's research showed that the things that make people satisfied and motivated on the job are fundamentally different from the things that make them dissatisfied. He asked office workers in Pittsburgh what made them unhappy at work. The list included low salaries, uncomfortable conditions, and poor management. These environmental factors, or hygiene factors, make people miserable and are demotivating – but their removal doesn't lead to intrinsic motivation. Instead, people are motivated by interesting work, the prospect of personal growth and self-actualisation, the thrill of meeting a challenge, and increasing responsibility.

But seeking analogies between corporate wage slaves and wealthy and pampered golfers is as misguided as it is patronising. It is enough to suggest that Herzberg's basic findings remain as valid today as they were in 1959 when he wrote his book, *The Motivation to Work*. Herzberg would conclude Jacklin's team didn't beat America because of cashmere and Concorde, but that he was a heck of a storyteller. His cashmere yarn remains a potent part of every European captain's armoury. When they lined up at Gleneagles in 2014, the European team caddies wore official cashmere sweaters for the first time.

Chapter 8

Year Zero

The 1980s was the transformative decade in the growth of the captain myth. It began in 1981 with business as usual: a one-sided American win. By the end of the decade Team USA was unrecognisable, and the confidence of the Palmer–Nicklaus years had been shattered by consecutive defeats at home and away. The upturning of the status quo in the 1980s led directly to the ascent of the captain – it was the moment he entered the media orbit in a substantive way. Tony Jacklin began leading before our very eyes. He rode on a golf buggy and talked into a walkie-talkie. The message that he was in charge was being conveyed; he was the agent of change. Suddenly, the captain was thrillingly decisive. He wore expensive sunglasses and was seen talking to subordinates while studying a clipboard. Rabble-rousing speeches were given and he was quoted by the business press keen to make sweeping analogies between sport and the corporate world.

For the first time, the American captain was held up to account by the golfing public and the media, who demanded answers for the decline in their team's performance. This prompted a period of introspection and infighting, the legacy of which remains in place today. The themes and divisions uncovered in the eighties were present in the questions underpinning Phil Mickelson's press conference rant at Gleneagles in 2014: do the Americans lack the hunger for the fight? Why doesn't the team seem to gel in the same way as the Europeans? Are they too greedy to play for a trophy which offers no direct financial reward? Is there something wrong with the American system that produces golfers who can become rich without needing to win? And, ultimately, are the leading European players just plain better than their American counterparts?

False Start

When did Europe become a team? The boring, literal answer to that question is 1979, when Great Britain and Ireland was expanded to include players from the rest of the continent. This wasn't Team Europe, the all-conquering love commune as we know it today, however.

'What are we doing here?' Seve Ballesteros asked Antonio Garrido as the prawn cocktails were handed round at one of the interminable pre-match dinners. 1979 was the new, Continental era's false start. Like a sunburned package-holidaymaker returning from Benidorm, captain John Jacobs was keen to show off his exotic Spanish trinkets, putting Ballesteros and Garrido out first on Friday morning against Lanny Wadkins and Larry Nelson. This was a big ask. The Americans had gone round the Greenbrier in 59 during practice the day before and they carried this form into the first match, reaching the turn in just 28 shots with their shared ball, with six birdies and an eagle, setting up a lead that was never overturned.

Wadkins and Nelson represented everything that was so intimidating about American golf through the 1960s and 1970s. Both have excellent Ryder Cup records and were cookie-cutter examples of the street-fighting matchplayers who populated American golf at this time. Their game was elevated by the competitive nature of the man-on-man format. Wadkins backed this up with a cocky arrogance that ran through American golf, sometimes greeting opponents on the first tee by shaking hands and saying, 'Hello, lunch.'

Both Wadkins and Nelson were present in Dave Marr's 1981 dream team, routinely described as the greatest ever version of Team USA, which thrashed Europe 18 ½ to 9 ½ at Walton Heath in Surrey, England. Nicklaus, Watson, Trevino, Floyd, Nelson, Irwin, Crenshaw, Kite: it was a team so full of stars that it made a pub quiz question of Bruce Lietzke – the only member of the team who didn't win a Major in his career.

'They were bloody good,' says Mark James, who was one of Europe's best players of the week, winning two points on the first day paired with Sandy Lyle. The gap in class between the teams seemed insurmountable, though. Paired against Jack Nicklaus and Tom Watson during the 1977 matches at Royal Lytham, James recalled, 'Nicklaus was such a good player then that if he hit a fade it moved about four feet left to right; if he hit a wild slice it moved 12 feet in the same direction. Watson was nearly as powerful as his partner, and I had never seen anyone with chipping ability quite like his.'

The European Idea Takes Shape

The real Team Europe, the version we would recognise today, began to take shape in 1983 – Year Zero – at Palm Beach Gardens, Florida. The match went down to the wire, with Lanny Wadkins again playing the role of the great American gunslinger, hitting a wedge to the final green to halve his match with José María Cañizares and secure a narrow American victory. 'Now it is a contest,' wrote David Davies in the *Guardian*. 'The European Ryder Cup team frightened the money-laden breeches off their American counterparts.' 'This score was no fluke,' said American captain Jack Nicklaus, whose idea it was to broaden the Great Britain and Ireland team into Team Europe in the late 1970s, a response to a long-held fear that the event was dying in the US.

Palm Beach in 1983 is where many of the tropes that have grown around captaincy were first aired. One of Jacklin's demands was for a dedicated team room at the course, a space that was fiercely guarded from interlopers. 'We knew that the team room was a vital thing,' said Jacklin of the 1983 match. 'It's hard to imagine that prior to then we were all left to our own devices in the evenings – other than the gala dinner – you could go off with your wife or your partner and have dinner in the town.'

With a team room, Jacklin said he was able to foster camaraderie, 'Something that you don't feel at any other time – there's nothing like it, you feel this responsibility. It's not just about you; it's about the 11 other guys and your captain. You dig deeper because of it. If you've got it in you, it comes out. I can promise you that.'

The team room was a media no-go zone, where the players could relax away from prying cameras and reporters. This only added to its allure, leaving the goings-on to the imagination, and apart from some recent Twitter intrusion, the legend of the team room has grown in the intervening years. Stories now 'emerge from the team room', and it has created a whole new category of player. For the first time, golfers were said to be 'good in the team room'. This brought a new Ryder Cup archetype, the team man, a catch-all for players who lacked stardust to merit a stereotype of their own, and gave captains something to say about players who had lost. In the binary world of Ryder Cup golf, where careers are defined by 1s and 0s, the team man was a rare qualitative measure, lending an extra dimension to doughty journeymen like José María Cañizares and Gordon J. Brand, who were cast as support players to the stars of the show, and there was no greater European hero than Severiano Ballesteros.

The 1983 match marked the second coming of Ballesteros, and the beginning of his journey to eventual sainthood at Medinah. Like all beatifications, Seve was required to provide an unsubstantiated miracle, which he duly delivered in his singles match against Fuzzy Zoeller. From a bunker on the 18th fairway, and out of range of the TV cameras, Ballesteros played 'the greatest shot never seen', the most talked about golf stroke since nobody saw Gene Sarazen hit 'the shot that went around the world' at the 1934 Masters.

With seven holes to play, Ballesteros was three up and seemingly on course to make his team's first point of the singles matches. Zoeller hit back with four consecutive holes before Seve holed a 20-foot birdie putt to take the match back to all square. Ballesteros hooked his tee shot on the 18th into thick rough, forcing him to hack out with a wedge, a shot that ended in a fairway bunker 250 yards from the green.

David Feherty's account captures the moment: 'Zoeller also found the rough with his drive, but his recovery made the fairway. He watched as Ballesteros stepped into the bunker with a 3-wood. It was total madness. With the lip of the bunker jutting up only feet in front, only a lunatic would attempt to hit such a shot with such a club. Ballesteros got settled, moulded himself to the contours, and with a swish of supernatural strength and grace, picked the ball clean off the top of the sand. It was jaw-dropping to everyone who witnessed it, except to the wizard himself, who was willing his ball on, spitting and hissing at it as it rolled onto the front of the green, 20 feet from the hole.'

Seve's shot from the bunker at the 18th was a moment of creative individual brilliance, the type of moment that has become central to the Team Europe narrative. Opposing captain Jack Nicklaus told reporters it was the greatest shot he'd ever seen and reflected that it was the kind of stroke he wished his team would play more often. Seve's miracle shot has been elevated over the years to become symbolic of the difference in the attitudes of the two teams. Europe's best players were at their peak during Ryder Cup week, whereas the Americans wear their national uniform heavily. More broadly, the 1983 match placed Ballesteros as the team's talisman, the emotional centre to Jacklin's cashmere and Concorde captain myth.

Who are We? A Usable Past

The All Blacks, New Zealand's national rugby union team, have one of the greatest records in all sport, winning 75 per cent of their matches over the last 100 years. In his book *Legacy, 15 Lessons in Leadership* James Kerr argues that the team's history and culture is a competitive advantage. 'You can't touch atmosphere, you can't see culture,' Kerr told *The Times*. 'But what you can see is behaviours. There are some very clear, direct things, like the role of leaders to select and create environments that people do their best in.' Every New Zealand coach borrows from the All Blacks' backstory – the team's myth – to create a sense of shared belief and common purpose.

This type of thinking is very fashionable among sports coaches who seek to use their team's backstory as a 'usable past', a phrase first coined by the historian Van Wyck Brooks. In this way, the past is not a passive compendium of dates and results, it is a bank of memories and stories that are weaved into a central narrative that moves history in one direction rather than another, making it feel inevitable.

Europe's usable past was clearly evident in Paul McGinley's captaincy for Gleneagles in 2014. The European team celebrated its successful backstory with images of former greats lining the walls of the team room. When he talked to the media, McGinley often referred to the issue of succession, suggesting that the teams of the past are linked to the present, and that there is a progression from one set of players to another. The message was that Team Europe had established a winning culture, a blueprint based on shared history that shaped the behaviour and norms of the current cohort. The subtext was that America was not just playing one team, it was up against a dynasty.

This is the story told by many of the great teams in sport. FC Barcelona, one of European football's iconic brands, works under the slogan 'more than a club' and often references its Catalan roots in the northern region of Spain where the club is based. As its mantra suggests, the club sees itself as representing values that reach beyond the football pitch – the club has been a high-profile supporter of the Catalonia region's fight for political independence and the defence of its own language and culture. The team has enjoyed enormous success over an extended period, becoming Spanish, European and World club champions. This has been achieved with a group of players such as Andrés Iniesta, Xavi, Lionel Messi and the captain Carles Puyol who were trained from a young age in the club's own youth academy, known as La Masia.

Likewise, 'The Yankee Way' captured how New York's baseball franchise was expected to perform in the 1940s and 1950s. The style of the team was said to pass down from senior to junior players. 'The Yankees were, to a man, a fiercely competitive group,' wrote Lew Paper, a player at that time, 'and they did not tolerate a teammate who seemed to be giving less than everything he had.' Paper called the team's attitude one of 'detached professionalism'.

'The Yankees had a philosophy that discipline doesn't come from the top,' he said. 'We disciplined each other. The expression heard all the time, especially when a veteran was talking to a younger player, was, "Stop fooling around. You're messing with my money." They were talking about World Series money, which we all needed badly.'

Like the All Blacks, Barcelona and the New York Yankees, the idea of Team Europe exists in the imaginations of the players, fans and media. What Jacklin created in the 1980s was still discernible nearly 30 years later at Gleneagles. The job of subsequent captains has been to carry the Team Europe story from one team to the next, creating one of the most intriguing examples of transition in modern sport.

In 1987 Europe won in America for the first time. Jacklin's status symbolism was backed by a new raft of sponsorship deals, which supplied his team with £500 cashmere jackets, and deals that sold spare capacity on Concorde for £5,000 a ticket, allowing the team and its entourage to go free.

Taken on its own, the 1987 result was hardly a shock. Running through Tony Jacklin's team was a spine of truly world-class players: Seve Ballesteros, Nick Faldo, Sandy Lyle, José María Olazábal and Bernhard Langer each won multiple Major championships in their careers, and Ian Woosnam won the Masters three years later, in 1991.

These six players were worked hard, with Jacklin using an approximate version of Pareto's 80–20 law, telling Bruce Critchley that he expected 60 to 70 per cent of the points to come from 50 per cent of the team. The big six played every series, with the minor characters filling in the gaps. A number of archetypes were created that remain in place today. José María Olazábal assumed the role occupied by Paul Way in 1983, cast as the Impressionable Youngster in need of guidance from a father figure – or, in Seve Ballesteros's case, more like a naughty uncle. Likewise, the version of Team Europe that captain José María Olazábal had at his disposal at Medinah in 2012 was also plenty talented enough for their victory to make perfect sense. The team contained four Major winners – Justin Rose, Rory McIlroy, Paul Lawrie and Graeme McDowell – along with two recent world number ones in Martin Kaymer and Luke Donald, the latter having headed both American and European money lists in 2011.

These two teams bookend a period in which Europe won eight times to America's four, and Team Europe has managed to do something that is the holy grail of team sport: Europe has made the transition from one group of players to another and maintained a winning record. Between Jacklin's '87 team, the first to win in

America, and Olazábal's 2012 vintage, Europe morphed from one group of players to another over the course of a quarter of a century. This despite existing for just one week every two years and, since 1995, being led by different captains on each occasion. Curtis Strange summed the process up well: 'Back in '83 we knew they were going to become a much better team with the involvement of European players, but we didn't know how good. We never anticipated just how good Seve, Sandy Lyle, Ian Woosnam, Bernhard Langer and Nick Faldo were going to be, and how long they would lead that team. That nucleus lasted for a long, long time. Sure, there were always a couple of new guys, but that was the nucleus that really made the Ryder Cup what it is today.'

Success has allowed Europe's teams to give the appearance of sharing a common culture, a way of doing things and an understanding as to the roles they are expected to inhabit. Europe's captains, bolstered by regular success, have, with very few exceptions, refused to break with traditions and norms set some 30 years ago.

Chapter 9

Our Heroes Define Us

Heroes symbolise the qualities we'd like to possess and the ambitions we want to satisfy, and nothing explains the difference between European and American golf more eloquently than their choice of talismen, Arnold Palmer and Severiano Ballesteros.

That both men were Ryder Cup captains – Arnie twice, in 1963 and 1975; and Seve in 1997 – seems hardly relevant. Instead they transcended the captaincy to become something closer to the teams' spiritual leaders, the people who help answer the question confronting all teams: who are we? And, just as importantly, who are they?

'Americans are a positive people,' wrote Barbara Ehrenreich in her book on the cult of positive thinking, *Smile or Die*. 'This is our reputation and our self-image. We smile a lot and are often baffled when people from other cultures don't return the favour. In the well-worn stereotype, we are upbeat, cheerful, optimistic and shallow, while foreigners are likely to be subtle, world-weary, and possibly decadent.'

These two stereotypes came together in the first round of the Suntory World Matchplay event at Wentworth in 1983. Arnold Palmer led Seve Ballesteros as they approached the final green. Palmer was 54 years of age and nearly 20 years past his last Major championship victory, whereas the 27-year-old Spaniard was in his prime, with two Masters and a British Open already to his name. The form book was also with the younger man, who won the matchplay five times between 1981 and 1991. Palmer had won the inaugural World Matchplay in 1964, and again in 1967, but owed his spot in the restricted field event to IMG, the company he had helped create with his long-time agent Mark McCormack. IMG owned the event, they sold the TV rights and sponsorship – they controlled the invite list.

The match was one of the very few times the two players went head to head in a competitive tournament, and this fact seemed to jolt Palmer to play some of his best golf in years, to the extent that the older man led by two holes with two to play. Ballesteros won the long par-5 17th to take it up the last hole, but seemed out of things going down Wentworth's famous 18th, another long par 5. Palmer was at the back of the green in three shots with a putt for birdie, while Seve was still some way short of the green in the line of the trees that overhang the fairway. What happened next was a piece of typical Seve magic, as he contrived to hole his 8-iron chip and run for an eagle three to halve the match and take it into a play-off which Ballesteros finally won at the third extra hole.

'I can't complain,' said Palmer later, when asked for his reactions to Seve's brilliant third shot on the 18th. 'For years I used to do the same to people.' It was a statement that encourages us to draw a comparison that has been made many times over the years. 'He was the backbone of the European Tour for so long. Seve was their Arnold Palmer,' said Curtis Strange when he heard of Ballesteros's premature death in 2011.

Palmer and Ballesteros, Arnie and Seve; each were the most charismatic golfers of their generation. Their peaks coincided with golf's boom years in America and Europe respectively – Palmer in the sixties and Ballesteros in the late 1970s and 1980s. They were handsome and telegenic and were famous beyond golf's natural constituency. Both were working-class boys done good, sons of golfing families who rose from the caddying classes to become the best players in the world.

'I'm very unpredictable and people see that,' Seve told Robert Green in 1985, attempting to explain his own appeal. 'I can go double bogey to eagle; make three birdies in a row and then three bogeys. People don't like to see somebody shoot par-par-par.'

It's a quote that could easily be substituted for use in a profile of Arnold Palmer, a figure so ubiquitous and so influential on American golf that it's easy to forget how good a golfer he was. Palmer won 60 times on the PGA Tour, a number bettered only by Sam Snead, Jack Nicklaus, Ben Hogan and Tiger Woods. Palmer's Major championship record also places him among the game's greats. His total of seven professional Majors is bettered by just six players. Between 1957 and 1971, he was placed in the top ten money winners on Tour for each year, winning a tournament every year from 1955 to 1971. Between 1960 and 1964 Palmer was elevated to 'king' status. In the 19 Majors, he won six, finished in the top five 14 times and in the top ten 16 times.

Seve's record is equally impressive. His tally of five Major championships consists of two Masters green jackets and three

Open Championship claret jugs. He was the first player in Europe to win £1 million, £2 million and £3 million in a single season.

Seve's Europe

European golf fans loved Seve Ballesteros for the same reasons that Americans found him infuriating: he was unpredictable, cunning and prone to emotional crises as well as outrageous highs. A key early scene in Seve's Ryder Cup story took place in the breakfast room at the Prince of Wales hotel in Southport in 1983. Having played for the first time in 1979, Ballesteros missed the 1981 match due to wrangles over appearance fees. So 1983 was when Ballesteros re-entered the Team Europe story, defined by Tony Jacklin as 'one of the key moments in Ryder Cup history'. Jacklin met with Ballesteros in an attempt to persuade him to play in that year's event at Palm Beach: 'It was an impossibility that he wouldn't be on our team,' wrote Jacklin. Seve was 'a virtuoso, a genius, not just a golfer, and he had that air to him of the passionate, tortured artist' and he shared Jacklin's antipathy towards both the mandarins of the Tour and to the greater enemy, America. Jacklin recalls the two men talked about how they had both been badly treated over appearance money and by jealous Americans who resented their talent. British fans want the chance to love you, said Jacklin, they want to get to know the real Severiano Ballesteros.

Well, as they say, good luck with that. As Dudley Doust wrote, Seve's mind was 'a private forest, a place impenetrable, indeed dangerous to others'.

Ballesteros's biographer Robert Green arguably knew him better than any other English-speaking journalist. Green worked with Seve on several book and film projects and spent many journeys, meals and downtime in the company of the player and his family. 'He was a complex character,' Green writes of Seve, 'Charming and manipulative, gregarious and withdrawn, open and suspicious, generous and mean – depending on how the mood took him.' Green's book title *Golf's Flawed Genius* captures his subject perfectly.

'Seve was very intense, very intense,' says José María Olazábal, shaking his head and laughing at the memory of his friend. Ballesteros and Olazábal were the 'best ever partnership in Ryder Cup history' according to Fred Couples, and it's hard to disagree. Together the Spanish pair played 15 matches, winning 11, halving two, losing two.

'He wanted to have everything under control,' says Olazábal of Seve's captaincy at Valderrama in 1997. 'He was almost telling the players how to hit their shots. Sometimes that created a little bit of friction with some of the players, for instance Monty, or Woosie. He was different, but he looked also at all the possibilities, you know, he had pairings, and saw how the Americans were playing – who was really strong in their team – and how he could set up the course. Who would have thought of putting rough in the middle of the fairway on 17 [laughs]? He was just making sure that everybody was going to be hitting the second shot from the same spot, you know . . . he was very intense.'

Olazábal was acutely aware of the legacy of Ballesteros on the next generation of golfers. 'Especially with the younger guys, maybe not so much with Woosie and Nick and all those guys, because they'd known each other for many years, but for the younger generations I think that he was crucial: the way he talked, because he made the players believe that they were good enough to win, and that is important. He gave them a belief. If the player was struggling he would approach the guy and look him in the eyes, saying, "It doesn't matter . . . it doesn't matter how you're playing. You just go out there and play your best and whatever that is that's fine with me, and you'll see . . . just make a few chips and few putts here and there and you will be able to win the match – at least keep the match as close as possible, as long as possible . . ." So he was important.'

Olazábal's reading of Seve's attitude chimes with his treatment of David Gilford in 1995. Seve's game was by then in the doldrums – his back injury meant he had become ever more erratic off the tee, increasing the need for a steady-as-you-go partner. Gilford fitted the bill perfectly, and captain Bernard Gallacher put the two together in the Friday afternoon fourballs against Peter Jacobsen and Brad Faxon.

'Seve was over straight away when the pairing was finalised, chatting and encouraging before we even went out,' remembered Tim Lees, Gilford's caddie. 'He knew he was hitting it all over the shop, left and right, didn't really know where the ball was going. He knew it was David who was going to be doing the hard work. On the first tee Seve put his arm around him and said, "Come on, David. You're the best player in the world. As long as you believe it, you're the best." Right away you could see David respond.'

The oddball partnership ended up winning 4 and 3, with Gilford, as predicted by Lees, 'doing the hard work'. On the long 13th hole the Englishman's ball came to rest on the edge of the deep fringe that surrounded the green. Ballesteros was again out of the hole, but was never going to go quietly – he used his putter to show Gilford the line, identifying a spot some ten feet left of the hole. Gilford rolled in the putt. 'It took what seemed an age to bend towards the hole and then dropped,' said Lees. 'As soon as it went in, the two of them hugged each other. In fact, Seve was so chuffed that he squeezed David so tight he knocked his hat off.'

Seve Versus America

Ballesteros helped define the line between them and us. And he really hated 'them'.

'In this group is the tournament leader, Seve Ballesteros from Spain,' said the announcer over the course tannoy at the Greater Greensboro Open in 1978, Seve's first pro event in the US. 'Let's give this spic a big Olé!' Welcome to America.

Seve's relationship with the country and many of its golfers was every bit as complicated as the rest of his life. 'I hear several times in the locker room, they say, "Here comes the Spaniard to take our money,"' he once told Robert Green. The suspicion was mutual. In his peerless biography of Seve, Green describes an incident on the first green at Muirfield Village in 1987, which captures the nature of the relationship between Ballesteros and a number of the leading American players of that time.

Seve had hit his approach to the first hole short and left of the green, about 40 feet from the pin. Olazábal was on the green, about 20 feet above the hole. Tom Kite, also on the green, had putted first and left his ball about three feet from the hole. Seve was next away but Seve – speaking in Spanish, reasonably enough – elected for Olazábal to go first with his difficult, slippery downhill putt, which he considered to be a harder shot than his chip. Olazábal left it short and went to mark his ball. Seve, again in Spanish, told him to putt out. The Americans, not understanding what was being said, asked what the heck was going on. Indeed, Curtis Strange seemed so discombobulated that he actually said, 'Can you speak Christian?'

Strange felt Olazábal might be on the 'comeback line' of his putt if he went on to putt out. Seve, this time in English, said: 'Don't worry. This is an easy chip. I'm going to hole it.' Which he did. After telling Olazábal to pick up his marker now that his putt was no longer needed, Seve said, 'Don't worry. Curtis isn't going to hole his putt anyway.' He didn't.

Strange was on consecutive losing American teams, in 1985 and 1987, as Europe's players exerted their dominance. The transformation in Europe's fortunes was down to the rise of the Seve generation of players at the captain's disposal. 'Jacklin was a good captain, but you have to say, "Right place, right time,"' says Strange. 'With Seve and those five great players – Faldo, Lyle, Langer, Woosnam and Olazábal – well, I just think they made Jacklin look fantastic. You have to give Seve an enormous amount of credit [for raising the profile of golf in Europe]. I loved him. It's like watching Mickelson today; you want to watch because you want to see when the train wreck is going to happen, to see how he is going to recover, and it was the same with Seve.'

Ballesteros, says Strange, was a great player who 'thrived on animosity . . . I played Seve seven times in the Ryder Cup and got my ass kicked virtually every time. You always had something going on out there, something happened out on the golf course that made you go, "Son of a bitch." What made me so damned mad was that I let him get to me. I like to see myself as something of a tough guy who doesn't let things bother me. But Seve bothered me. And I got pissed off at myself because I let him get under my skin. It was the crap, the gamesmanship. You knew it was coming but it still bothered you. Seve knew the buttons to push. That's the beauty of matchplay. I love the gamesmanship, it doesn't bother me one bit. But it bothered me with Seve. There's a little shit going on all the time. Over the years there's always something happening out there, certainly with Seve, and with Nick [Faldo].'

Strange remembers giving some advice to then teammate Paul Azinger before his fellow American played Ballesteros in a singles match at the Belfry in 1989. 'I took him [Azinger] aside and said, "Don't you let him fuck with you! Don't even look at him, don't watch one swing of his. Just leave him alone!"' Strange laughs at the recollection. 'Sure enough, twice over 18 holes they were at each other's throats, certainly on the last hole they had a confrontation. Azinger came back into the locker room and said, "Man, you were right about him."'

Azinger learnt fast. His previous experience of Seve was of a charming and encouraging playing companion during the US Open. 'What a gent,' thought 'Zinger' as Seve kept urging him to keep concentrating to the end of the round.

A few years later, after a series of tussles in the Ryder Cup, Azinger's view had moved closer to that of Strange, labelling Seve the 'King of Gamesmanship' after the 1991 match, a comment aimed at highlighting Ballesteros's box of tricks, which included a tendency to cough at strategically important moments in a game. Such was Seve's reputation in the American camp that on his debut in 1993 Davis Love was given a pack of lozenges by a group of the American players' wives, should the Spaniard be afflicted during their foursomes match.

What was Arnie Selling?

If Ballesteros gave Team Europe its emotional centre, then Arnold Palmer carried out a similar role for Team USA in the 1950s and 1960s. More than any other single figure in American golf, Palmer defined what it meant to be an American golfer. 'We wanted to be like Arnie,' says Raymond Floyd. 'He showed us the way.'

Where Ballesteros was a dark, brooding and complex character, Arnie told a simpler, less ambiguous story – he has done more than any other player to provide American golf with its social, moral and political compass. His enduring legacy, says Raymond Floyd, can be gauged by his influence on the way American golfers of following generations defined themselves as versions of him. Before Palmer defined the role, America's golfing heroes were very different men, says Floyd; they were harder and much less congenial. 'Hogan, Snead, Dickinson and those guys were – how should we say it? crusty,' says Floyd, chuckling. 'That's it, they were crusty.'

Boxing, American football and baseball had been transformed by the exposure of television – golf, however, was a harder sell. It had been televised on a sporadic basis since the early fifties, but it was hardly love at first sight. The players were dull and grey by comparison to the superstars available elsewhere on the dial.

Palmer's arrival coincided with America's love affair with television. In 1950, only 8 per cent of American families owned a TV set. By 1960, Palmer's *annus mirabilis*, that number was 88 per cent, and the box in the corner had moved to the heart of American life. 'The right man at the right time,' said Nicklaus.

'I don't know why anyone would go to a golf tournament. The prices are inflated, they don't let you in the clubhouse and you can't see a thing,' said Ben Hogan, summing up his generation's attitude to the idea of golf as entertainment. Just as Bob Harlow had created the Walter Hagen story, so much of the Arnie brand was manufactured by a master of spin, in Palmer's case Mark McCormack, the creator of IMG.

The work paid off in spades, making Palmer very rich indeed, to the extent he remains one of golf's top earners today, still gracing magazine covers, the subject of adoring feature interviews. It's testimony to Palmer's likeability and McCormack's PR nous that his great wealth has never driven a wedge between the star and his constituency of fans, even a group as committed as Arnie's Army.

With such raw material at his disposal McCormack set to work selling Arnie to corporate America. 'How uncomplicated, I think to myself, the job of representing a golfer must have been back when only golf was involved,' wrote McCormack in 1967. He wasn't kidding. After shaking hands on a deal to start IMG with Palmer, McCormack built a global business empire that remains at the core of the golf business today. His description of a typical week in the life of Arnold Palmer around 1964 reveals the extent to which he sweated sport's most valuable asset. 'On Monday morning Arnold appears at a studio for the filming of colour television commercials for Noxzema. The company is putting out a line of products called Swing – maybe. Test marketings have to go well. A small fortune is at stake . . .'

By Tuesday afternoon the filming is done. Arnold hurries to La Guardia and flies in his jet to Shawnee, Pennsylvania, to participate in the grand opening of a food-processing plant built by his father-in-law, Martin Walzer. He spends the night in Shawnee. The next morning he flies back to New York City, where he picks up four top business executives and flies them to Latrobe for a VIP day of golf, meals and drinks at Laurel Valley Golf Club. On Thursday he poses for photographs again, this time for the Bolens Division of FMC, for whom he endorses lawn equipment and snowploughs . . .'

McCormack always balanced any business story with the 'good ol' Arnie' narrative which references Palmer's small town, blue collar roots back in Latrobe. 'No matter how big his world may be, he is small town,' McCormack told *Sports Illustrated* in 1967. Arnie's own heroes were traditional American people, Palmer told Thomas Hauser, 'men like Dwight Eisenhower, John Wayne, Bob Hope'. Norman Rockwell painted his portrait and his famed affability meant he was as popular with presidents as he was with Pittsburgh steel workers. 'If I could go back in time and meet people I've never met,' Arnie said, 'I'd like to meet the Wright brothers, Charles Lindbergh and Will Rogers. And going back further, I'd like to know if there really was a Robin Hood in Sherwood Forest, and if there was, what was he like?'

Like many men who lived through the Great Depression, Deacon Palmer, Arnie's father, was a Democrat. 'He thought Roosevelt hung the moon,' said Arnie, 'but I'm the opposite. I think you solve problems through family and personal charity. The less big government and big-name outsiders get involved, the better it is for us all. All Dwight Eisenhower ever wanted was to make America the ideal place to be.'

Despite Walter Hagen's attempts to gentrify the job of the PGA professional, most remained blue collar, union men who were expected to know their place in the country club caste system. This was certainly the lot of Palmer's father, Deacon, who was greenkeeper and head pro at Latrobe Country Club in

Pennsylvania. 'Palmer didn't want his father's life, the life of a club pro,' wrote Ian O'Connor in *Arnie and Jack*. 'A man spent too much time being demeaned in that life, being treated like a towel boy by hundreds of country club snobs.' Palmer helped his father around the place – 'The worst worker I ever gave a job to,' Deacon told anyone who'd listen. As the pro's son, young Arnie was a notch above the caddies in terms of privileges, meaning he could play the course in the evenings when the members were gone for the night.

Perhaps the greatest achievement of Arnold Palmer's business career is that the boy who wasn't allowed on the course now owns it. Yet for all the Arnie teashops, launderettes, snowploughs, golf clubs and umbrella-branded T-shirts, Palmer was selling much more than that, he was selling a version of America.

The European Incentive

The stories of Palmer and Ballesteros have left a legacy that is directly relevant to the captaincy. Put simply, the Europeans have a greater financial incentive to first qualify, and then play well at, the Ryder Cup.

When Europe wins, a common reading is that their players 'want it more' says leading golf psychologist Bob Rotella. The reason is the Ryder Cup plays a far larger role in the ultimate judgement of a player's career. 'When the American press writes down who the great players are, they don't list the Ryder Cup in their list of achievements,' says Rotella. 'There is more of that in Europe. Look at Colin Montgomerie, for example, he will go down as one of the greatest players in history, and some of that is because of what he did in the Ryder Cup. You see it in the adoration Seve gets, or even Sergio García. If you didn't win Majors in America, you are probably not going to go down as a great player. You certainly won't be regarded as such because you were a good Ryder Cup player.'

Push Rotella's point further and another incentive becomes clear: the Europeans have more to gain financially from success at a Ryder Cup. Again, this is central to the role of the captain and of the issue of motivation of the players in each team room. Palmer's multi-billion dollar brand was built on the back of his performances as an individual player, in Major championships and on the PGA Tour. Ballesteros, meanwhile, owes a great deal of his fame and the affection with which he is held to his appearances in the Ryder Cup. This is particularly true of his relationship with the British golf audience, who hero-worshipped Seve as one of their own throughout the golf boom of the eighties and nineties. The lesson of Seve's career is that qualification for the Ryder Cup team is more valuable to European players than it is to Americans.

Money is always a sensitive topic at a Ryder Cup. For one week in 104, 24 of the world's wealthiest sportsmen play for (very generous) expenses only. The absence of prize money encourages the view that the Cup is about something more, such as a higher calling to team and country. Whenever the subject of pay-for-play is brought up, the golfer concerned faces the backlash of faux outrage by those who claim the soul of the event would be corrupted. In the week running into Brookline in 1999, David Duval was quoted as saying that the Ryder Cup was an 'overcooked' event, little more than an exhibition. It was a line that was to come back to haunt him as critics noted Duval's readiness to play Tiger Woods in a sponsored head-to-head match in California which carried a prize fund of more than £1 million. On the first morning at Brookline, an American voice welcomed Duval to the first tee: 'Hey, David, play your ranking.' When Europe took the early lead in the match, the home crowd was quick to link what they saw as America's underperformance with the money issue. 'What kind of exhibition is this?' said one, and, 'How much you being paid to play like this?'

The Ryder Cup is bigger than David Duval, said Bernard Gallacher, the three-time European captain. 'It shows that our heart is in playing for Europe in the Ryder Cup, whereas the likes of Woods, [Mark] O'Meara and Duval are more interested in the big bucks. Maybe that's why we've been so successful in recent years.'

Incentives come in many guises. In his first Ryder Cup, Darren Clarke was playing for more than pride. At Valderrama in 1997, the 2016 captain was drawn against Phil Mickelson in the singles, having won his previous fourball match on Saturday morning playing with Colin Montgomerie against Love and Couples. The Clarke–Mickelson match went to the 17th , where the American rolled in a five-foot putt to halve the hole and win the match 2 and 1. A point for America and a $180,000 hit for Clarke, the cost of a new Ferrari F40, which he'd have taken home had he won.

The bonus deal had been arranged between Clarke's agent Andrew 'Chubby' Chandler and the player's then clubmakers, MacGregor. If Clarke went through the week with a perfect 100 per cent win record the car would be his. 'I actually wasn't thinking about that when we went out to play – well, not much,' wrote Clarke in his autobiography. 'It was somewhere in the back of my mind, I suppose. But Phil, as Phil can so often do, chipped in a couple of times, played very nicely and beat me on the 17th.

MacGregor were spared their bonus, although I don't think they would have minded handing over the keys, and not just for the coverage they would have received.'

The story of Darren Clarke's Ferrari is a less than subtle example of using the Ryder Cup's global profile to make money. This is a process that has become more sophisticated.

Since 2008 Ian Poulter has inhabited the Ballesteros role as the leader in the locker room and the team's emotional heartbeat. Like Seve, Poulter has a tribe all of his own. Go to the local muni and there is every chance you will see a host of mini-me's strutting off the first tee in garish check trousers, sunglasses, visors, gel in their hair. This is how the sports business works: we watch the stars on television and then follow them to the shops. Faldo had his own devotees, all Pringle jumpers and flyaway fringes. The baby boom generation were Palmer men. They wore chinos and Penguin polo shirts, the uniform of the American country club. For the last decade, local golf courses have been full of Tiger's tribe: Nike's Swoosh covering them from cap to toe.

The Seve image used at Medinah talked to a generation of British golf fans for whom his victory at the 1984 Open Championship at St Andrews was one of the key moments of European golf boom. As they watched his fist-pumping victory celebration on the 18th green – the pose that was captured on the sleeve of Team Europe's clothing – thousands of young men noted the navy blue Slazenger v-neck, white shirt and white shoes, which coalesced into the Ballesteros brand. The comparisons are telling because in brand terms Seve was keeping company with the very biggest names in the world of golf. He just wasn't making as much money as they were.

Palmer's business partner Mark McCormack regarded Seve as the one that got away. 'I'd like to have signed Seve Ballesteros, for sure, at the beginning of his career,' McCormack told *Golf International* magazine in 1999. 'As wonderful as he is, as charismatic, as talented, the package of Seve Ballesteros would have been a better one with us [IMG] managing him than it's been with others. So I'm sad about that.'

While Ballesteros was a rich man by most standards, his income was a fraction of other players'. As Robert Green points out, Seve was never listed in the annual *Golf Digest* ranking of the game's top 50 earners. In 2006, the year of the Spaniard's retirement from competitive golf, Tiger Woods made $86 million and Arnold Palmer and Greg Norman – both some way beyond their peak playing years – made more than $20 million in the year. The last name on the list made £3.3 million, suggesting Ballesteros's income was less than this.

Greg Norman, the 'Great White Shark', was Seve's great rival through the 1980s. Like Palmer, Norman's approach to business was a world away from Seve's. 'As an athlete, you are a pass-through entity,' said Norman. 'Agents were taking commission on an annual basis and if you had a three-year deal to represent someone they would take their money and you knew there would be another Greg Norman down the line. There was, he was Tiger Woods.'

Rather than rent his Great White Shark brand to the highest bidder, Norman created his own intellectual property and then licensed it to companies operating in markets as diverse as grass seed, beef cattle, wine and clothing. Given how much money he has made, it's little surprise that it is Norman's business model rather than Seve's that is being copied by the best of the present generation of players.

Unlike Seve, Ian Poulter is comfortable talking business models and brand equity, subjects on which he is every bit as knowledgeable as he is on the golf swing. 'Greg Norman is a big role model, also Faldo,' Poulter said during an interview at his home Woburn club in England, a month before Medinah. 'If we go back a few years I would look at the Greg Norman collection when I was working in the pro shop, helping to choose some of the kit for the shop. Going from that to playing with him, to becoming a good friend of his and getting to know him really well, he inspired me to become better at golf and in business.'

A few weeks after Medinah, the European Tour's official Ryder Cup clothing supplier Glenmuir, began selling a special, limited edition '2012 Ryder Cup Seve Tribute Box Set'. The company's press release gave the details of the deal: 'Priced £150, the sequentially numbered box sets each contain a high quality Glenmuir navy lambswool jumper and white cotton polo shirt with the Official 2012 Ryder Cup Match Shield embroidered on the chest and the unique "Seve Tribute" embroidery on the left arm . . . It is identical to the embroidery worn by the 12 players who produced the greatest European comeback in Ryder Cup history to win 14½ – 13½ during the "Miracle at Medinah" in Chicago.' The company's marketing director said he expected the initiative would raise over £120,000 for vital cancer research in Seve's name: 'During the Ryder Cup we received thousands of enquiries from golfers trying to buy Seve's Sunday colours, navy sweaters and white shirts, with the iconic embroidery worn by the European Team – and now they can.'

The irony of Glenmuir selling Seve-branded merchandise would not have been lost on the man himself. When the same company used Ballesteros's image to advertise its Ryder Cup range in 1990, Ken Schofield of the European Tour and John Lindsey the head of the British PGA (as rights holders to the Ryder Cup) received a warning letter from the player's then agent, Joe Collet. Seve had sold his name and face to several other clothing companies around the world, which conflicted with Glenmuir's use of his image. Why should he wear the official Ryder Cup uniform in future if it was causing him such trouble with the people who were paying for his services?

The sad aspect of the celebration of Seve at Medinah was the unseemly squabble over the ownership of the Ballesteros name. When he died, Seve left 90 per cent of his wealth to his three children, who also control the Severiano Ballesteros Foundation, which is 'dedicated to nurturing young golfing talents and supporting research into brain cancer'. So powerful is the image of Seve that it became embroiled in the expensive and deeply political game of bidding to host the 2018 Ryder Cup. A few weeks after his death, the Ballesteros family put the iconic family name behind the Tres Cantos course, north of Madrid, which was up against rival bids from France, Germany, the Netherlands and Portugal. 'It would be the greatest tribute to him,' Baldomero Ballesteros said at his brother's funeral. 'I appeal to the sensitivity of the Ryder Cup committee of the European Tour to agree the greatest honour that could be bestowed on Seve is to award the competition to Spain. I appeal on behalf of the family.' This created a deeply sensitive issue for the European Tour, as they had decided to award the 2018 event to Paris. A compromise was mooted by several players, including Pádraig Harrington, Nick Faldo and Colin Montgomerie, who suggested the Tour adopt the famous Seve silhouette image as its corporate logo.

Like all great icons, his tragic death has merely enhanced the power of the Severiano Ballesteros name. He also highlights a central point in the difference between leadership and management. Seve's effectiveness as a captain in 1997 may be open to interpretation. Even his best friends smile at the recollection of his frenzied approach to the role. But that he was one of the great leaders in the history of European golf is inarguable. The job title is irrelevant.

Chapter 10

Hunger Games

As American dominance of the Ryder Cup began to slip in the mid-1980s, Jack Nicklaus and Arnold Palmer went in search of something to blame. They chose money. There was, thought the two richest golfers in the world, just too much of it around. The decline in the American team's performance coincided with a huge hike in prize money available on the PGA Tour. This was no coincidence said Jack and Arnie, it was a simple matter of cause and effect.

In 1985, an American Ryder Cup team lost for the first time since Palmer's friend Dwight Eisenhower was in the White House. Two years later, he endured the sight of an American team, led by Nicklaus, lose at home for the first time ever. The new world rankings system, which had been created by Palmer's mentor Mark McCormack in 1985, confirmed the player's suspicion that the best golfers in the world were foreigners. Greg Norman, Nick Faldo, Seve Ballesteros, Bernhard Langer and Nick Price dominated the top of the rankings for much of the 1980s and early

1990s. By comparison, thought Palmer, American players had grown soft on prize money that was way beyond the dreams of players of his own generation.

Worse still, they didn't have to win to become rich. 'In 1954, the year I turned pro, the total prize money on the PGA Tour for the entire year was $600,819,' wrote Palmer in the USGA annual report. 'I had to win to make a good living. Now, fast forward to 1992. In a single year, Fred Couples won $1,344,188. Twenty-two golfers had more than $600,000 in official Tour earnings. In fact, one player won $609,273 in 1992 without winning a tournament.' In 1960 the total purse on the PGA Tour was $1,335,000. Ten years later it was $6,750,000, and by 1980 it had reached $13,370,000, ten times what it was 30 years previously. Between 1983 and 1987 the prize money virtually doubled from $17,600,000 to $32,100,00. This huge hike in cash corresponds exactly with the decline in America's fortunes in the Ryder Cup. Palmer let rip: 'These are very skilled golfers; and most of them are very nice men. But the money has taken away their hunger, and they aren't following the road that leads to being a hero.'

When America lost at Muirfield Village in 1987, Jack Nicklaus used the defeat to make the same point. 'There are a lot of players who sit on our money list from about 30 to 200 who will say, "There goes Nicklaus again,"' he said on the Sunday of the 1987 defeat. 'But I'm going to keep on preaching. You've got to have winners, you've got to have heroes, and you've got to have superstars that people look at.'

Winners he said, got the job done when the going got tough down the stretch. He pointed to his team's inability to close out Jacklin's European team, who won every match that went down Muirfield Village's 18th hole. 'Instead of being aggressive,

American pros develop a percentage type of style,' said Nicklaus. 'On the European Tour, there is less competition, which puts players in contention more often and makes them better, more aggressive finishers.' He didn't mention him by name, but one player on the 1987 team seemed to sum up Nicklaus's argument.

The Dan Pohl Problem

By the time his career was over on the PGA Tour, Dan Pohl had amassed 70 top-ten finishes and made more than $3.1 million. Over this period he won just two tournaments, both in 1986, which under the qualification rules America operated at the time, was enough for him to make Jack's 1987 team.

Throughout '87 – the second year of qualification – Pohl had played well enough to win the Vardon Trophy, awarded to the golfer with the lowest adjusted scoring average over a minimum of 60 rounds. That Pohl achieved this feat without once winning a tournament, had not escaped Nicklaus's attention.

What's more, Pohl had some form when it came to blowing it when the going got tough. He was a popular figure on the Tour, but rarely contended in the Major championships, the ultimate test of nerve outside of the Ryder Cup. The closest he came was at the Masters in 1982, and it hadn't ended well. He'd played his way into second place on Sunday afternoon, still some way behind the eventual winner Craig Stadler. The threat posed by Pohl was summed up Stadler's then wife, Sue, who said to a friend on the course, 'Isn't it nice that Dan Pohl is playing so well?' Pohl was safely in the clubhouse when Stadler started 'dripping oil', to use the player's own phrase, bogeying three of five holes to cut his four-shot lead to one. 'The Walrus' needed to par Augusta's final hole to win, but three-putted, meaning Pohl was now in a play-off for a green jacket.

As the pair went down the first play-off hole, the tenth, Pohl made a hash of his chip from the fringe and left himself an eight-footer for a half. He missed. 'I tried to jam it in and simply didn't make it,' he said later. 'Would Johnny Miller say I choked my guts out?' he said. 'Probably. Because that's the kind of thing he says.' Pohl's weekend total of 134 was four shots better than anyone else's in the field. He was one of only four players to shoot under 140 over the final two rounds. 'I had nothing to be disappointed about, nothing to be demoralised about,' he said later.

Five years later Pohl was paired with Hal Sutton in the first morning foursomes at Muirfield Village against the strong European pair of Ken Brown and Bernhard Langer, the first time he had played the format in his life. Length off the tee was Pohl's greatest strength, and after a dropped shot at the first hole he dovetailed with Sutton's excellent iron play. After a morale-boosting 18-foot par putt on the second hole, Pohl was up and running. He and Sutton ran out 2 and 1 winners and were paired again that afternoon against Faldo and Woosnam. This time they lost, with Pohl missing a putt on the 17th green to end the match. Nicklaus had seen enough and sat Pohl out for the whole of Saturday, pairing Sutton with Larry Mize for both formats.

Europe led the 1987 match by 10½ to 5½ going into the final day's singles, an unprecedented lead based on Tony Jacklin's strategy of using his 'big dogs' over the first two days: past and future Major winners such as Langer, Lyle, Olazábal, Faldo, Woosnam and, of course, Ballesteros. These were just the sort of men that Nicklaus wanted in his team, the type who didn't buckle when the heat of competition was at its most intense.

America started on Sunday needing to win nine of the 12 singles matches, a feat that would have been a greater comeback than either Brookline or Medinah. They might have pulled it off too, were it not for their failure to close matches on the final hole. Of eight games that went down to the 18th, Europe won three and halved five. America did not win a single match on the 18th green.

In Nicklaus's eyes this was evidence that his team had a soft underbelly. Men like Pohl, Larry Mize and Andy Bean seemed to embody what Nicklaus saw as the problem with what he called the 'American system', one that produced players who made a lot of money but lacked the 'winning mentality'.

In the final day's singles, Pohl was drawn against the Englishman Howard Clark. Both players struggled for form and carded matching 75s, three over par. 'It was like pulling teeth out there,' said Clark later.

Pohl made a par on the second hole to take the lead and then promptly lost it again on the third, never to regain it over the course of a match of very low quality. The players matched bogeys and pars throughout the scrappy round and were all square going down the 18th, where Clark hit a 310-yard drive leaving him a 7-iron to the green. Pohl hit a loose tee shot that ended up in a fairway bunker, from which he could only progress the ball to 30 yards short of the green. With Clark close to the green in two, Pohl hit a horrible skulled wedge shot for his third, flying through the green and coming to rest in another bunker. From there he took three more shots to make a double bogey six to lose the match one down.

'Some guys on the Tour live and die golf. I'm not one of them,' said Pohl later. 'Frankly, if there was a way to make the living

I make now without playing golf, I might go for it. I'd rather be out working in the yard pruning the trees or pulling up the weeds than thinking about hitting four buckets of balls.'

It was not the sort of thing you would expect to hear from Jack Nicklaus, but to be fair to Dan Pohl he wasn't the only player to disappoint the Golden Bear. Larry Mize was another player who failed the test. His surprise victory in that year's Masters was only the second win of his pro career (his first had been at the 1983 Danny Thomas Memphis Classic). Mize led Sam Torrance by one hole on the 17th tee only to find water and end up with just a half. Andy Bean was also caught in Jack's crosshairs: 'I know this course probably better than anyone,' fumed the captain, 'yet not one of my team has asked me for advice about what shot to play, or which club to use. If Andy Bean had asked me when he pulled out his 9-iron on the 17th, I would have knocked it out of his hands.'

The failures of Pohl, Mize, Bean and others played to Nicklaus's argument that the European Tour was producing better players. He painted Ballesteros, Faldo and Langer as products of a hothouse environment that forced them to become battle hardened by going head-to-head down the straight on a more regular basis than their American counterparts. Winning golf tournaments, thought Nicklaus, was a habit and in this sense the Europeans resembled the American players of a previous era, when Snead, Hogan et al. drove from town to town playing in winner-takes-all tournaments. By comparison, he said, the current version of Team USA consisted of a 'bunch of guys who get the most out of their games, but we just don't have the kind of player with the game that can be dominant. And I don't see one emerging right away.'

Compare Nicklaus's gloomy analysis of American players with that of Bernard Gallacher two decades earlier: 'Let's not kid ourselves, America produces tough, determined golfers: it's the hardest school in the world. The competition is terrific, it takes plenty of guts to play well over there.' Gallacher was talking after the 1969 match at Birkdale where he had partnered Brian Huggett in a fiery fourball encounter with Ken Still and Dave Hill. That 1969 American team was led by Sam Snead and featured many of the hard men Nicklaus was suggesting had been lost to the PGA Tour.

'I thank God I have this gift to play golf,' said Ken Still. 'I've come from nothing, eaten from paper-covered tables. This is our livelihood, it's tough, we are all tough pros.'

Money, though, was still hugely loaded in America's favour, to the extent that going into the 1969 match every American player had won more money that season than any of the Great Britain and Ireland players had won in their careers to date.

The Two Jacks

Jack Nicklaus is a central character in the story of the Ryder Cup. He helped keep the Cup alive in the dark days of the 1970s and early 1980s, when America's complete dominance was undermining fan and media interest in the event in the US. It was also Nicklaus who is credited with persuading the British PGA to include players from Continental Europe in 1979, which allowed Seve Ballesteros, Bernhard Langer, José María Olazábal and countless other superstar Europeans to play in the event, a move which evened the talent pools supplying the teams.

Jack Nicklaus's role in the concession at Royal Birkdale in 1969 is arguably the single most important story of the many that go into making up Ryder Cup history. The concession story gives the event its point of difference in the oversupplied market for professional sport where, outside of the four Major championships, merit is measured by the size of the cheque, and golfing talent is quantified by the money lists on both sides of the Atlantic. To gain the attention of the best players, Tour event promoters compete to offer the biggest prize purse. At the FedEx Cup, the PGA Tour's end of season event, the winner takes home north of $10 million.

Given this backdrop, the Ryder Cup's story is pleasingly counterintuitive, and whenever a player dares suggest being paid to play in the event, he is firmly directed back to the concession at Birkdale, the nuts and bolts of which are familiar to every golf fan.

The 1969 match was a snarky, niggly affair and the two teams were tied as the final singles match between Tony Jacklin and Jack Nicklaus headed down the 18th fairway.

Jacklin was slightly longer off the tee, leaving Nicklaus to hit into the green first, which he did, manipulating his ball to the centre of the large green, some 25 feet from the hole. Playing second, Jacklin overhit his 8-iron approach, running through to the back of the green, some 30 feet away. The Englishman had made a long eagle putt of a similar length to tie the match on the 17th, but this time he left it short, leaving Nicklaus a putt for the Ryder Cup. The Golden Bear missed and ran it four feet past, taking it beyond Jacklin's ball, meaning the American had not lost his turn and now had a four-footer to save the Cup. He made it and picked up Jacklin's marker to concede the putt, holding his hand out to shake hands. The match was halved without the need for Jacklin to make his putt.

'I'm amazed at the attention that got because at the time I didn't think it was a big deal,' said Nicklaus, years later. 'I simply thought it was the right thing to do. It didn't make any difference to the result because we were going to retain the Cup either way, so I didn't want to take the chance that he might miss the putt and have his stature diminished. Tony was a hero and, as the then Open champion, was so important to the game of golf in Britain.'

This quote is of the type we have come to expect from Jack Nicklaus. It shows a generosity and broad emotional intelligence of someone able to grasp that there is more to life than golf, and more to golf than getting the ball in the hole. This is post-concession Jack talking, however. There are two Jacks that populate golf history, and they are separated by that afternoon on the north coast of England in 1969.

From Fat Jack to Arnie-lite

Born in Ohio in 1941, the young Jack was a natural sportsman. Aged 13 he stood 5 foot 10, weighed 165 pounds and ran the 100-yard dash in 11 seconds flat. He was the starting quarter-back for his junior high school football team, and its punter and placekicker. For the basketball team he averaged 18 points a match and once made 26 free throws in a row, garnering prizes and awards. On the golf course he was marked out early as the next greatest player in the world. As a young teen phenomenon he won every local event going with a power game that left caddies and competitors shaking their heads in disbelief. 'The crack, the boom,' recalled his college teammate Dow Reichley to

Ian O'Connor in *Arnie and Jack*. The noise made by a Nicklaus drive 'was a supersonic sound'.

After winning his first US Amateur in 1959 aged 18, Nicklaus emerged as a public figure at the 1960 US Open at Cherry Hills, Colorado. The event was won by Arnold Palmer and Nicklaus's 282 total was the best aggregate score by an amateur in US Open history. 'I didn't win, nobody ever remembers who finished second at anything,' he said after the round.

The first of his 18 Major championships was the 1962 US Open Championship, in which he overcame Palmer at Oakmont Country Club, in Pittsburgh's north-east suburbs. This win summed up the marketing challenge that faced the pre-concession Nicklaus. Oakmont was prime Palmer country. America's favourite golfing son grew up a few miles away in Latrobe, and the steelworkers from the Pittsburgh area made up a sizeable chunk of Arnie's Army, his devoted band of fans. 'Americans demand villains for their heroes to slay,' wrote Thomas Hauser of that week in Oakmont, 'and Jack was a storybook rival for Palmer.'

Arnold was perceived as having succeeded at golf the hard way. Although being the son of a club pro was hardly a disadvantage, he'd been a fighter all his life. Nicklaus, by contrast, was seen as having been given the world on a silver platter, born into a wealthy family and members of one of Ohio's most exclusive country clubs. Nicklaus had enormous raw potential that had been moulded by the best teachers and golf coaches his father's money could buy. Hauser contrasted Jack's background with that of Palmer: 'After Arnie and Winnie eloped, they'd lived in a trailer. When Nicklaus and his fiancée, Barbara Bash, got married, his parents gave them a down payment for a house.' Arnold was a 'regular guy' whereas Nicklaus was a 'whale with a computer heart' who moved around the golf course slowly and deliberately 'like a German housewife picking lint off a suit'.

The barbs about his weight and his personality were hard to brush off. 'Everyone likes to think of himself as a basically appealing fellow,' said Nicklaus. 'I know I do. Being as honest as I can, I think of myself as fundamentally companionable; a shade more sensitive than I appear to be, a bit too direct on occasion, a bit too stubborn on others; but a good deal less cold and grim and cocksure than some people read me as being. I'm aware that I'm not the matinée idol type. Rooms don't light up when I enter. And I'd be less than candid if I didn't say that there have been moments when I wished I'd come up when golf had a less glamorous idol.'

In the months after Birkdale, Nicklaus underwent a rebrand. He was, he said, tired of wearing the black hat, of being the villain to Palmer's superhero. The concession was the transformational moment in Nicklaus's story. After 1969 it was as if he were born anew. A few months after the concession he left IMG to set up on his own. He didn't want to play second fiddle to Palmer for Mark McCormack's attention. 'Jack had begun to remake himself in what many believed was the image of Arnold Palmer,' wrote Hauser. A diet and exercise regime meant he'd dropped 25 pounds, including six inches from his hips. 'His hair had grown long; even the shape of his face seemed to have changed.'

The young Nicklaus, the country club brat, would likely have stood there waiting for Tony Jacklin to miss his putt on the 18th because 'nobody remembers who came second', after all. The pre-concession Jack might have seen generosity as a weakness, a view that would have been shared by the 1969 American captain

Sam Snead, who accused Nicklaus of showboating when he came back into the locker room that day. Snead was not impressed at being the first American captain not to win the Ryder Cup outright since 1959, and only the third in the entire history of the event.

'Wait, what's he doing?' said teammate Frank Beard, as he saw Nicklaus picking up Jacklin's marker. 'Oh we were irate. I was, for sure,' wrote Beard in 1992. 'It may have been a great gesture for Jack, but the other 11 of us had worked very hard and wanted to win. He just arrogantly assumed that the team and the country, individually and together, would want him to make this sporting gesture.' Jacklin, said Beard, should have been made to 'show us he could make a four-footer with the weight of a whole nation on his shoulders'. Captain Snead agreed. 'I would never have given a putt like that, except maybe to my brother,' he said.

For Nicklaus, however, the concession at Birkdale altered the trajectory of his career. He was still a winner, but he was becoming likeable too. Jack's concession was the sort of gesture Arnie would have made. And to American golf fans, there was no higher compliment.

But there is a postscript to Jack Nicklaus's relationship with the Ryder Cup, which adds a different perspective to his role in the story of the event since the concession at Birkdale. It's also a reminder of the political background to professional golf that shapes the environment every captain must work within.

Jack Nicklaus's captain myth was derailed by the defeat in his own backyard in 1987, which followed the narrow victory four years earlier at Palm Beach in 1983. This was not how Jack's Ryder Cup story was supposed to go, and it was an embarrassment that at the time he tried to deflect, using the argument that increases in prize money on the PGA Tour had contributed to the decline in quality of the US Ryder Cup team. Yet behind the scenes, Nicklaus and Palmer were furious at what they saw as the PGA Tour's encroachment into their own commercial interests away from the course. This led to a peculiar double standard. In public, Jack was presenting himself as the guardian of American golf, the man seeking to protect standards, whilst behind the scenes, he was seeking to take over the PGA Tour and run it on behalf of himself and a small coterie of other star players.

'I'll do everything in my power to stop that man,' said Jack Nicklaus, sitting in Arnold Palmer's office at Bay Hill Club and Lodge in March 1983. Outside, crowds of spectators were starting to file through the gates for that day's pro-am, the curtain raiser to the annual PGA Tour tournament starting later in the week. Inside Palmer's office, the focus of the conversation was Deane Beman, the 'Czar of golf' who, in the opinion of Nicklaus, was overstepping the mark in his role as commissioner of the PGA Tour.

The meeting between golf's two most famous players was part of a plot to overthrow Beman and take greater control of the money now flowing into the PGA Tour. Nicklaus's plan was for a handful of the biggest stars to take over and run it in their own interests. The new Tour would be made up of a smaller number of the very best players. Sponsors and television, said Nicklaus, would line up to buy in to see the best of the best play against each other outside the auspices of the PGA Tour, leaving the Czar with a devalued product made up of journeymen and unknowns.

Aware of Palmer's great commercial clout and influence among the players, Nicklaus used the meeting at Bay Hill to persuade the King to sign up to what amounted to a coup aimed at unseating Beman. With Palmer on board, Nicklaus had the credibility to sell his idea to the other star players, which he did over the course of the 1983 season.

A former pro golfer and friend of Nicklaus, Deane Beman was commissioner of the PGA Tour from 1974 to 1994, a period of rapid and unprecedented financial growth. On Beman's watch, the professional game in America enjoyed greater television coverage, increased commercial income from sponsors and TV rights fees leading to massive hikes in prize money. This all sounded great, but to Nicklaus and Palmer, Beman was part of the problem not the solution. They had set up their own companies in order to take advantage of the growing corporate interest in golf. They thought the money that Beman was generating for the Tour should be going to them. It was they who generated the interest, it was they who got the turnstiles clicking, and it was they who should be rewarded with sponsorship money.

Beman was now the enemy who needed to be put back in his box, or if Nicklaus was to have his way, removed from office entirely. In the eyes of the very best players, the administrators of the Tours are little men whose job is to assemble the schedule and prepare the courses. Not surprisingly, Beman saw things differently. 'Nicklaus looked at business the same way as he did a golf competition: for every dollar one side made, the other side had to suffer a loss,' wrote Beman in his autobiography, *Golf's Driving Force*. 'That there could be more than one winner in the same contest was as foreign to professional golfers as conceding a five-foot putt.'

As Beman extended the commercial reach of the PGA Tour, so he trod on the toes of the best players. The Tour should, in Jack's opinion, be limited in the types of sponsorship deals it could do so as not to infringe on the players' own commercial rights. A dollar spent on a Tour sponsorship was a dollar they wouldn't spend to be on the cap of Nicklaus, Palmer, Tom Watson or any of the top stars of the game. If the Tour signed Coca-Cola as an official partner, why would they need to pay Tom Watson to endorse their product? They didn't, and dropped Watson as an endorser in 1983. The irritation felt by Watson was still raw a decade later when he summed up his view of the conflict in a *Golf Digest* interview: 'I think the basic problem is that the Tour is competing with its own players, but at the disadvantage of the successful players who could go out and market their own image.'

Sponsorship money was small fry compared to that on offer in the market for golf course design. By the early 1980s Nicklaus, Palmer and Watson had their own design businesses and were furious when Beman and the PGA Tour entered the market with an audacious real estate deal. Beman paid one dollar for a 415-acre piece of land in Sawgrass, Florida, from a developer who had fallen behind on his mortgage payments. The site became the TPC Sawgrass, the headquarters for the Tour and the home course to its flagship event, the Tournament Players' Championship, complete with its iconic island green on the 17th hole.

A golf course built and designed by the Tour represented several million dollars that wouldn't be going to Golden Bear Inc. In 1977, Jack's company employed 178 people across several divisions, selling a product portfolio that ran from golf clubs, bags and balls to car dealerships, a travel agency, a radio station, cattle ranches, real estate developments, a natural gas company and golf course architecture.

Word of rebellion in the ranks reached Beman at an otherwise routine meeting of the PGA Tour tournament policy board on 17 May in Atlanta, where that week's Atlanta Classic was being staged. Beman was saved by the veteran Tour player and committee member, Jim Colbert, who leaked the fact that revolution was in the air to the board. Colbert, an old friend of Beman's, had got a whiff of the story when he sat in on a meeting of the players in the locker room at the Byron Nelson Classic a few weeks before. He had listened as Nicklaus outlined his objections to the room full of players, including many of the leading stars of the game. Nicklaus had sought, and got, the backing of the top players, who signed a joint letter demanding the head of Deane Beman for 'getting into their business'.

Beman's defence to Nicklaus's accusation was that everyone benefited from his efforts to grow the game, and particularly the star names. 'If the pie grew bigger they would still be the top chefs. They would still have their pick of the plums,' wrote Beman. The issue came to a head with a letter sent to Edward de Windt, the chairman of the tournament policy board, signed by 12 of the biggest stars of the PGA Tour, including Nicklaus, Palmer and Watson, along with Ben Crenshaw, Gary Player, Craig Stadler, Hale Irwin, Raymond Floyd, Johnny Miller, Lanny Wadkins, Lee Trevino, Tom Weiskopf and Andy Bean.

Beman was shaken by the names on the letter, some of whom he had previously felt were his friends and allies. But his reputation as a hard man with an eye for detail was well earned. Having studied the letter, he noticed one sentence that was to seal his victory in stamping out Nicklaus's rebellion. The letter alleged that he and the board had 'exceeded its mandate' and that the commercial activities were 'unauthorised'. Both of these points were untrue, and what's more Beman had a piece of paper to prove it, complete with the names of Jack Nicklaus and Arnold Palmer at the bottom, giving their explicit permission to expand the Tour's commercial activities. Nicklaus had overstepped the mark, and Beman forced him into a humiliating backdown at a meeting of the players at the end of the season.

'It couldn't be a mediation,' wrote Beman. 'It had to be a conceded putt by a formidable competitor and sportsman. Jack saw that he was dead wrong. He was trapped by his own words in the letter and his previous actions as a board member. He realised he patently had a serious PR issue. He had something to lose.'

Nicklaus stood up at a pre-arranged meeting with the Tour players, where he looked them in the eye and said he'd been wrong to go against Beman. 'I think I'll stick to golf for a while,' said Nicklaus, as he left the locker room. Jack's tussles with Beman were a reminder of the *realpolitik* surrounding the captaincy. The administrators of the game on both sides of the Atlantic manipulate the system within which the captain operates, working the machine against which our heroes rage. The captain has a number of motivational levers at his disposal but they pale when put against those at the disposal of the Tours and the PGA of America. This has been the case since 1927. To the players and their agents, the administrators are petty bureaucrats, grey men in blue blazers who hide behind consensus and committee decisions, running the back office that arranges the event schedule and makes sure the cheques are in the post.

A more balanced view is that the game's administrators have been a necessary counterbalance to the selfish agendas of the superstars and their agents. 'The single most difficult issue of the Ryder Cup is finding the balance between the authorities and the stars of the game on both sides of the Atlantic,' says Keith Waters, European Tour Chief Operating Officer. What is certain is the blazers have proved themselves every bit as tough a bunch of competitors as the best matchplayers.

Chapter 11

The Big Mo

Mark James first felt it about two hours in.

The final day's singles matches were progressing and the European captain was walking between holes, making notes on club selections as his players passed through the two par 3s on Brookline's front nine, the second and seventh holes.

His assistants Ken Brown and Sam Torrance were keeping tabs on the other groups, picking up information on clubbing and green speeds that could be relayed back to the later starters. The wind had changed, altering the nature of the course, playing havoc with club selection. Over the first two days Lee Westwood and Darren Clarke had chosen to hit 3-irons into the seventh green. On Sunday the hole was downwind, and in his opening singles match against Tom Lehman, Westwood had gone with a 7-iron.

These changes duly noted, James wandered back down the course to pick up Jesper Parnevik's match against David Duval. The pair were playing the par-4 fourth hole, and the Swedish player was deliberating over his approach, talking it over with his caddie, Lance Ten Broeck.

James looked beyond the players to the large leaderboard on the other side of the fairway. It was 'painting a picture I didn't care for' said James, in his trademark tone of wry understatement. 'There was a sea of USA red, and it was not my favourite colour . . . we were rapidly going under, and nobody seemed to be throwing any lifejackets our way.' The madness had begun.

3 and 2
4 and 2
4 and 3
6 and 5
3 and 2
5 and 4

To its advocates, this is what momentum looks like.

These numbers represent the scores of the first six Sunday singles matches at Brookline in 1999, all of which went America's way. Over the course of five hours Tom Lehman beat Lee Westwood, Hal Sutton won against Darren Clarke, Phil Mickelson outclassed Jarmo Sandelin, Davis Love thrashed Jean Van de Velde, Tiger Woods beat Andrew Coltart and David Duval overcame Jesper Parnevik.

Tom Lehman recalled the exhilaration of that afternoon: 'You had to have seen the scoreboard. It was all red. And not just red but big red. It was 1 up, 2 up, 3 up, 4 up in every match. All red. Duval was 4 up, 5 up, 6 up. Davis was 5 up, 6 up. It was a whuppin'.'

The session set Mark James's Bad Captain story in stone as the man who got on the wrong side of momentum, sport's most mysterious force. Since that afternoon in 1999, momentum has been elevated to the single most discussed area of Ryder Cup strategy. It is one of the first questions asked at every press conference, and underpins many of the captain's decisions, from team order and pairings, to wildcard selection and even course set-up. Everyone wants to know who has got it, how to get it if you haven't got it, and what to do if it's coming straight at you.

The short version of the Brookline story is a mirror image of the four-point turnaround witnessed in 2012 at Medinah. Captain Ben Crenshaw's team turned a four-point deficit on Saturday evening into a one-point victory come Sunday afternoon. America trailed Europe 10–6 when Lee Westwood hit the opening tee shot in the first singles match against Tom Lehman. When the day was over, Team USA were 14½ to 13½ to the good.

It wasn't until later in the afternoon that Europe scored their first point of the day, when Pádraig Harrington beat Mark O'Meara one up. Steve Pate then beat Miguel Ángel Jiménez and Jim Furyk overcame Sergio García, leaving the US just half a point short of reclaiming the Cup.

With three of the final four matches out on the course Justin Leonard holed a monster putt on the 17th green against José María Olazábal which prompted many of the American team and some of their entourage of supporters, wives and caddies to rush onto the green to celebrate. Olazábal was left with a putt of similar length to that just holed by Leonard to keep Europe in it. He missed and the match was over.

This is a pared-down description of a highly charged and controversial day of golf. It's not going too far to say that it was the day the captaincy changed, and remains very influential in terms of the effect it has had on the strategy and decision-making of the captains on both sides.

The problem is that while we know what happened at Brookline, we're still not sure why.

Very Nearly the Best Captain Europe Ever Had

From the moment his team landed in Chicago on Sunday night, Mark James barely put a foot wrong, winning virtually every tactical battle on and off the course. He had been seen in some quarters as a controversial choice to lead the team, having been a divisive figure 20 years previously during his second match as a Ryder Cup player, at the Greenbrier in 1979. James, along with his friend Ken Brown, were fined on their return from America for a series of misdemeanours and failures of etiquette. As a result of his early run-ins with authority, the outlaw Mark 'Jesse' James made some high-profile enemies along the way to Brookline, most notably two of Europe's biggest stars, Tony Jacklin and Nick Faldo.

Captaincy, he said, was 'something I'd had done to me in the past', which coloured his view of the role. In James's view the job of captain was to take as much of the pressure off the players as possible in what is a 'peculiar week'. The regular routine of many players on the European Tour sees them arrive at the event venue on Tuesday evening for a Thursday morning tee-off. Commercial pressures mean that Ryder Cup week is a different-shaped animal, with time taken up by official dinners, sponsor and media engagements and speeches from local politicians, business people and celebrities. When it came to playing golf, said James, well, that's what golfers do, right?' 'I was not needed to hold their hands or cut their fruit at breakfast, and I could see no reason to practise captaincy while they practised golf.'

James's 1999 team was one of the least experienced in terms of Ryder Cup appearances that Europe had ever put out, with seven rookies in the side. Conscious of this inexperience, James took care to emphasise areas that he saw were fundamental to effective Ryder Cup game strategy. For example, he warned his team against charging the first putt four feet past, 'because when the Ryder Cup heat is turned up, putts of that length seem immeasurably longer'. Such nuggets were drilled into the players in the early part of the week; avoiding three putts became one of James's mantras.

He noted other things that could have tripped up the unaware. He warned of the shift in tempo between the first two days of foursomes and fourball play and the singles matches on Sunday. Likewise, the need to keep loose, particularly in foursomes, when players can go for a hole or two without playing as many shots as they would in a normal round. There would be no curfews or alcohol bans. The underlying message was that these were professional people who, for the rest of the year, managed their own affairs. 'I was dealing with adults and they knew what to do and what was best for their games,' said James. 'My job was simply to ensure that mentally they were OK, in the right pairings and looked after properly by all and sundry.'

The practice days saw James experimenting with pairings and monitoring form. Paul Lawrie, who had won that year's Open Championship at Carnoustie, was paired with fellow Scot Colin Montgomerie. Another debutant, Sergio García, went out with Swede Jesper Parnevik, and Lee Westwood and Darren Clarke took their close friendship off the course to the tee.

James's main concern was the form of José María Olazábal, the two-time Masters champion, who came into the week struggling with an errant driver that undermined the initial game plan to pair him with fellow Spaniard Miguel Ángel Jiménez. An alternative presented itself, however, in the shape of Irishman Pádraig Harrington, who was hitting the ball beautifully and seemed to have the perfect game for the first morning foursomes. Both Jiménez and Harrington were playing their first Ryder Cups, but James didn't agree with the received wisdom that rookies are better off under the protective wing of a gnarled Cup veteran, particularly on the first day when nerves and the shock of the new are at their most extreme. 'In my experience, experience is overrated,' said James at the press conference ahead of the first day.

When the match got started, Europe had the better of the opening encounters on Friday morning, when Montgomerie and Lawrie beat David Duval and Phil Mickelson 3 and 2 while the Parnevik and García combination was proving an inspired choice, beating Tiger Woods and Tom Lehman 2 and 1. The pair went unbeaten for their four matches, winning against Phil Mickelson and David Duval in the Friday afternoon fourballs, and then followed up with a 3 and 2 victory over Payne Stewart and Justin Leonard on Saturday morning. Only a half against Love and Duval in the Saturday afternoon fourballs prevented Parnevik and García from a 100 per cent record through the week.

This was a partnership that showed James's captaincy at its best. Today, in his post-playing career as a TV commentator for the BBC, he has a reputation as one of the best analysts on the golf circuit. Back then he had noted the early rise of Sergio García as the next big thing when the player had won the British Amateur

Championship in his teens. In particular James admired Sergio's ability with the driver and the quality of his iron play, which was exceptional. García also had a natural exuberance that captured James's imagination. That type of brio can energise a team room if harnessed in the right way. García wanted to be partnered with Parnevik, another for whom James had a soft spot. It wasn't Parnevik's famed eccentricity off the course that James liked, it was his style of play on it. 'His game has no holes, and few hit the ball straighter. I thought he would be the perfect foil [for García].'

By the end of the Saturday afternoon fourballs, the four-point lead established on day one had been maintained and Europe led America 10–6. No team had ever turned over four points on the final day and James was basking in the light of a job nearly well done: 'The consensus view on Saturday evening was that I was a pretty good captain,' he said.

The Day that Changed the Captaincy

The criticism of James is focused on his team order for the singles, and the decision to keep three of his team on the sidelines throughout the first two days. 'It was obvious that Ben [Crenshaw] would load his top order – he had to in order to stand any chance at all,' says James. Armed with this assumption, James hedged, putting two experienced players at one and two – Lee Westwood and Darren Clarke – followed by three players who were yet to hit a ball in anger: Jarmo Sandelin, Jean Van de Velde and Andrew Coltart. 'If either of Clarke and Westwood had made a point we would have won the Cup,' said James.

As a consequence of Mark James's pairings over the first two days, three of the first six players out on Sunday – Westwood,

Clarke and Parnevik – were playing their fifth match of the week, raising the issue of burn out. Each of the player's caddies was sure that mental and physical fatigue played a big role in their defeats. 'Lee [Westwood] didn't play all that well, and that was a pity as we were first out,' said Mick Doran, his caddie that week. 'Lehman played all right; Lee just couldn't get into it. He didn't tell me he was tired, but I did wonder. You just never know how you are affected mentally.'

Darren Clarke's physical condition was also questioned by his bagman on that day, Billy Foster: 'It seemed to be a case of, "Stand up and be counted and fall over the line . . ." Darren was shattered. He'd be the first to admit it. He played quite poorly, really. He won the first hole, chipped in, and was psyched up for it – but whatever he tried, he couldn't pull anything off. Sutton played steadily and beat him.' Likewise, Jesper Parnevik's caddie Lance Ten Broeck also felt exhaustion was a factor in his man's poor showing on Sunday: 'Oh yes, he was tired all right. I didn't think he was physically tired; but mentally he was done in.'

The balance of how many matches one player can play has frequently been a major decision point for the captains.

In 2008 Paul Azinger pointed out that, statistically, players who play all five matches lose in singles more than 75 per cent of the time. Despite these odds, Azinger played Phil Mickelson in all five matches at Valhalla: 'Five matches in a Ryder Cup is tough, and I couldn't fault Phil for running on fumes by Sunday afternoon.' As previously mentioned, in 2012 Davis Love benched Mickelson on Saturday afternoon despite the player's 100 per cent record to that point, the idea being to rest Mickelson for the singles and to make room for other players.

The record books are not much help in establishing what is or isn't the right strategy, and there is plenty of contradictory evidence that playing the best players in all five matches can work.

The matches were played over 36 holes until 1961, when the format was changed to four matches of 18 holes, still over two days, Saturday and Sunday. That 1961 match was won by the USA by 14½ points to 9½. The shorter matches were aimed at helping the British and Irish team, but of the seven matches that reached the 18th hole with the outcome still at stake, two were halved and the other five were won by the USA. In 1983, Tom Watson asked captain Jack Nicklaus if he could sit out a session, as he was playing less than his best. 'Listen,' said Nicklaus, 'whether you're 70 per cent fit or 100 per cent, it doesn't make any difference. The intimidation factor is there, and you will step onto that tee in every fight.' It was Watson who played the deciding match against Bernard Gallacher, securing the point needed by America to win the match 14½ to 13½. In the same match, Tony Jacklin told Gordon J. Brand he would be sitting out the first two days, while the pair were sitting on Concorde flying over for the match, part of Jacklin's strategy of basing his pairings around Europe's big dogs, who routinely played five games out of five to great success.

The superior fitness of today's players should mean that the decision is less of a factor for the captain than it was in Arnie's day. At East Lake Country Club, Atlanta, in 1963, home captain Palmer – the last playing captain – noted the superior fitness and work ethic of his team. He used the results from the afternoon sessions as evidence of this assumption. In the three morning sessions – the matches had extended to Sunday for the first time – Great Britain and Ireland held their own, tying 8–8. But the afternoon sessions were their undoing, going down 15 points to one after lunch. The British did not record a single victory from the three afternoon matches, the single point coming from two halves. 'I think our boys worked harder,' said Palmer. 'Whenever our players were not on the course, they were practising, while the British stayed around the clubhouse.'

At Brookline Crenshaw said he was taken aback by James's decision to put in his three untried players early. 'We knew they'd lead off with Clarke and Westwood, but what they did next (at three, four and five) surprised us,' wrote Crenshaw later. 'We thought he would sprinkle them around. But this? To put those three players together that early in the line-up was probably a lot to ask.'

America's first six made for a formidable line-up: Tom Lehman, Hal Sutton, Phil Mickelson, Davis Love, Tiger Woods and David Duval each won their matches before the 17th green. Yet how Ben Crenshaw got to this order is a bit murky. His assistant captain Bill Rogers maintains that the team meeting on Saturday night saw Crenshaw at his finest, playing the democratic captain, gesticulating and poring over the options, cigarette in hand. Tom Lehman said that the original line-up presented by the management team had Tiger Woods in tenth spot, contrary to the momentum strategy subsequently claimed. 'We all said, "Hey, if we're going to win this thing, we're gonna have to get on them early and get on them hard,"' Lehman later told *Golf Digest*.

According to Jim Furyk a number of the senior players, such as Davis Love and Hal Sutton, were central to the line-up decisions, whereas Mike Hicks, Payne Stewart's caddie, painted a different picture: 'There were seven or eight captains around the table that night. Guys were saying, "I should play here." Mickelson said, "I think I should go off first." It was very unlike other Ryder

Cups. It easily could have led to chaos.' Mark O'Meara's account plays it down the middle: 'Mickelson and Davis were really talking about strategy, what they wanted to do and what they thought would work. The rest of us just kind of sat around. I kept my mouth shut, because I'd played in only one match and got beat.' Future captain Davis Love recalled seeing the lists for the Sunday singles go up on the noticeboard in the team's hotel: 'Guys started saying, "Hey, we can win the first six! It can happen!"'

Flexibility was Mark James's mantra for his week as captain. 'I wanted us to remain open to ideas and events as they happened rather than go in with a rigid dogmatic idea of how we were going to play and line up,' he said. In reality this meant that when things went well on the first morning, James kept his pairings more or less together through the foursomes and fourball matches of the first two days. This decision more than any other formed Mark James's Bad Captain narrative. 'Many people have come out and criticised me over the years for not playing every member of the team before Sunday,' says James. 'It's a very mundane and obvious criticism in many ways. But there's a fair chance that if I'd have broken up a winning team we wouldn't have been four points up on Saturday night, and I would have been the mug. So you can't win, really.'

Andrew Coltart's caddie that week was Ricci Roberts, a long-time caddie for Ernie Els. He recalled Mark James giving Coltart the news on Saturday morning that he was not going to be playing that afternoon. 'I tried to console Andrew,' said Roberts. 'He was extremely disappointed that he wasn't going to be playing until the singles.' Roberts was sympathetic to what he called James's 'Catch-22', of changing winning combinations, but pointed out that James had picked Coltart as a wildcard. 'Why didn't he go for Langer if he was going to do something like that?' said Roberts.

Given their antagonistic history, it was less surprising that former captain Tony Jacklin put the blame for defeat on James's strategy: 'I looked at the pairings with Peter Oosterhuis and I said, "Shit, if these first two guys get beaten, they've given all of the game away." Of course, it happened exactly like that. If James had gone in there with Montgomerie and Parnevik and the strength from the off, they'd have blasted them out of the water.'

The Herd Mentality

Recent captains have adopted the language of the money markets to help them explain what they saw on Sunday at Brookline and, later, at Medinah. 'Brookline was the first time I can recall people using the term "momentum" to talk about the fluctuations in a match', says Ian Woosnam.

In financial circles, markets have always been prone to *Manias, Panics and Crashes*, the title of Charles P. Kindleberger's masterly book on the topic of financial instability. History is full of examples of investors being swept along by the excitement of those around them, leading to many of the biggest financial crises – from the Dutch tulip bulb collapse of the 1600s and the South Sea Bubble of 1720 through to the 2000 dotcom crash and the banking collapse of 2007. Each of these 'bubbles' was the result of herd behaviour, in which investors – both individuals and institutions – blindly and irrationally followed those around them only to panic sell when the market turned against them.

In his book, *The Big Mo: Why Momentum Now Rules Our World*, former derivatives trader Mark Roeder wrote about what it felt like to be in the grip of momentum when buying and selling shares on the stock exchange: 'It emerges stealthily rather than arriving suddenly. It creeps up and envelops us, and we are often not aware of it until it has already made an impact. Momentum often feels good, at least in the initial phases. It is seductive. There is a feeling of moving forward, of getting somewhere. It can be thrilling to go with the flow.'

Roeder's description of momentum in the financial markets is very close to the way golfers describe their experience of flow during the Ryder Cup.

'Momentum is like the wind,' says Paul Azinger, down the phone from Florida. 'Seriously, I'm standing here outside and it's just come to me. I've had an epiphany: it's like the wind, you can't see it but you can feel it, and it's really powerful.'

'You feel helpless,' said Mark James, of his experience on that Sunday at Brookline in 1999. 'The only thing I could do was to meet them at the par 3s and give them some clubbing advice, and try to just be there to answer questions and offer help. But really it's down to the players. There's not much you can do when the round is ongoing. That lack of control is really scary.'

Transferred to Brookline, the momentum argument assumes that there is a causal link between Lee Westwood losing to Tom Lehman and Darren Clarke being defeated by Hal Sutton. Because neither Westwood nor Clarke scored a point, momentum assumes it was harder for Jarmo Sandelin to beat Phil Mickelson and this, in turn, reduced Jean Van de Velde's chances of winning against Davis Love. And so on through the card. As the first four matches went America's way, it became more likely that Andrew Coltart's would fall to Tiger Woods and that Jesper Parnevik would be beaten by David Duval.

The counter-view is that momentum is a figment of the golfer's imagination. It wasn't momentum that caused America to overturn Europe's four-point lead on the final day as there is no causal link between the matches, which are stationary, or isolated, events. Instead, the results of the matches on that Sunday in '99 – and at Medinah in 2012 – were merely an example of the laws of probability in action. America and Europe were regressing to their 'mean performance'. Having played below expectations over the course of the first two days, those first six American players were due a better performance, and it came on Sunday afternoon.

'Whether there is such a thing as momentum is up for question,' says Dr Jim Taylor, a renowned performance psychologist who has worked with professional golfers. 'The data is very uncertain. Momentum is a bit like luck. It gives random events a sense of controllability. When there's a change in direction in a match – i.e. when someone starts to play better or worse – we say there's been a change in momentum. But that one shot, or a single victory or a run of good play, can be explained by the natural swings in performance. Golfers need to feel like they are in control so they create a force called "momentum" to help explain random events.'

The definitive research into the subject was carried out by Professor Thomas Gilovich of Cornell University, for a paper that appeared in the *Cognitive Psychology* journal in 1985. Its title was 'The Hot Hand in Basketball: On the Misperception of Random Sequences'. In it Gilovich attempted to find out whether a player who had hit a basket with their last shot was more likely to hit it with their next one, a phenomenon known as 'streak shooting' or the 'hot hand'. Gilovich reported that 91 per cent of fans agreed that a player has 'a better chance of making a shot after having just made his last two or three shots than he does after having just missed his last two or three shots'. This is not true, said Gilovich, and to prove it he followed the Philadelphia 76ers for a season, tracking the results of their free-throw shooters. Gilovich's findings told him that players who had hit their last one, two or three shots were no more likely to hit their next than players who had missed their last one, two or three. In fact, they were slightly less likely: the weighted average of 51 per cent hits after a hit, compared to 54 per cent after a miss.

It's easy to get tricked into thinking we're on a roll when we're not, says Dr Taylor. 'If you look at a small period of time, let's say a few holes, someone can hit a remarkable shot, or series of shots, and we can think that it represents a change in momentum. But if you look at that shot in the context of the dozens or hundreds of shots made in a Ryder Cup match it is not that remarkable, it doesn't indicate that dramatic a change.'

The law of averages, however doesn't make such a good story, and the job of journalists is to help readers make sense of the chaos. Viewed in this way, the momentum story is largely a product of humanity's inability to detect randomness or, more accurately, our over-eagerness to detect patterns.

More than any single Ryder Cup before or since, Brookline shaped how captains viewed their job. If momentum was the key factor, then the captain could attempt to manipulate it in his team's favour. Since '99 the captain is often viewed as the agent of change, further raising the perceived importance of the role. The problem with this view, as outlined by Mark Roeder, is that it encourages people with authority – politicians, business leaders, Ryder Cup captains – to do things 'because they believe they have momentum on their side . . . the pros and cons of their decisions become less relevant than the momentum factor.'

Maybe. There are people who believe absolutely that the world is flat, says Dr Jim Taylor. 'But that doesn't make it so.'

Chapter 12

What Went Right?

The questions surrounding momentum are central to the captain myth because they talk to the issue of his relevance. Does he matter? Do his decisions impact on his team's performance and the result of the match? Or is he a high-profile non-entity who is powerless in the face of forces beyond his control?

At its core, the momentum story is about change. Sports fans, journalists and commentators routinely use momentum to help explain what they are watching. Flick through the sports sections of the daily papers and the momentum story is alive and well in the lexicon of sports reporting. In the hands of a skilled writer it adds pace and direction to an otherwise unconnected series of events, or string of matches, and is a useful narrative trope.

Brookline and Medinah bookend a period in which momentum became the single most discussed area of the captain's strategy. Both saw a four-point turnaround on Sunday, the biggest comebacks in the event's history and, in both cases, a shift in momentum was most commonly cited as the reason for the change in fortunes, for America in 1999 and for Europe 13 years later.

At Brookline, the start of the story was Europe's early success over days one and two. The end of the story was America's dramatic victory on Sunday afternoon. As at Medinah, what is less clear is what caused the tides to turn. If momentum shifted, when did it happen? Why did the mysterious force move from one direction to the other?

There are plenty of opinions on the subject. Was it captain Ben Crenshaw's performance at the Saturday evening press conference, in which he wagged his finger and said fate would decide the following day? Or was it Team USA's motivational meeting that evening, which included a cast of characters as diverse as Pamela Anderson, R. E. M., President George W. Bush and cheerleaders of the Dallas Cowboys?

Ben Crenshaw's own account of events puts Colin Montgomerie in the frame for inadvertently winding up the Americans and spurring them on to greater efforts the following day. Crenshaw recalled Julius Mason (PGA head of communications) walking into the team room on Saturday night with the day's quote sheets and transcripts from the European press conferences. 'One quote on the sheet jumped out – one from Colin [Montgomerie]. "You know we've won, don't you? It's silent. Great, and that's the best thing we can do – silence the crowd by outplaying them."' Crenshaw claimed that Monty's comment fired up a number of his team, while Monty denies ever saying it at all. A similar point is made concerning Johnny Miller's criticism of Justin Leonard, the man who holed the monster putt that sealed America's win on the 17th green against José María Olazábal.

Leonard had struggled with his game earlier in the week and a key moment came at the halfway point on Saturday, when Crenshaw was under pressure to change his team around. The captains must submit the afternoon pairs before the morning foursomes have finished, and Crenshaw was debating the issue over a walkie-talkie with his vice-captain Bill Rogers and Bruce 'Leaky' Lietzke, who were out on the course with some of the players. 'Tell Ben I want to go back out,' said Leonard to Lietzke, who relayed the message to the captain. 'My hunch is that Justin Leonard should go home and watch television,' said Miller, live on NBC, when he saw the afternoon pairings. 'The guys heard about that on Saturday night and, well, let's just say it was one more thing to motivate us,' said Crenshaw. 'Like we didn't have enough already.'

Other factors have been put forward as being pivotal to the momentum swing on Sunday. As we've seen, Mark James's singles order and his decision to keep three of his players on the sidelines for the first two days regularly gets an airing; as does the stacking of the American top order. The latent anger said to reside in the American team room after the pay-for-play issue dominated the run-in to the event is also considered to have played its part.

Each of the above reasons has been cited as the missing link between the start of the story and the climax. The same question can be asked of the events at Medinah in 2012. The shift from America to Europe is often put down to Ian Poulter. For most of that Saturday session it had been business as usual, with America in the driving seat. At 5.46 p.m. Dustin Johnson and Matt Kuchar finished off Nicolas Colsaerts and Paul Lawrie to put America 10 points to 4 up and seemingly out of sight. The penultimate match looked like good news for the home team too. Having trailed García and Luke Donald by four shots at the turn, Woods and Steve Stricker were threatening to pull off a great comeback. At the 18th Stricker had an eight-foot putt to steal a half, only to see the ball roll past the hole, 10–5 to USA.

Enter 'Poults', the self-styled postman, because he always delivers. Teamed with McIlroy in the fourball match against Dufner and Johnson, the Englishman birdied the final five holes to win the game one up. The cameras captured Poulter's wide-eyed, fist-pumping celebrations on the final green as the player was engulfed by his teammates.

'We have a pulse,' said Poulter as he entered the team room that evening. 'It was the first good vibe we felt that week,' said Jamie Spence, who runs Team Europe's back office.

Poulter's brilliant run of birdies on Saturday afternoon gave the plot its twist. Before that moment the match was an American walkover. After Poulter's scene it became the European fightback.

The first five singles matches out on Sunday were won by Europe. By 3.28 p.m. the four-point lead America had held overnight had gone, and it was fitting that Poulter was the man at the controls when parity was achieved. He overcame Webb Simpson on the final green to claim his fourth point from four starts.

'Making five birdies on the Sunday when the momentum is with you is one thing, but what Ian Poulter did in making five birdies in a row on the back of Rory making one on 13 is incredible,' said Paul McGinley, who cited Poulter's play at Medinah when selecting the out of form English player as one of his wildcard picks for Gleneagles in 2014. 'That was a monumental achievement and there is no doubt he personally pulled the team into a position to be just within touching distance.'

During press briefings throughout his tenure, European captain McGinley used momentum to frame the discussion. 'The first two days in Medinah we got hammered. We were on the ropes,' said McGinley, who was vice-captain to José María Olazábal in 2012. 'I saw that sometimes you put good strategies in place, you have the players well prepared, but sometimes when you're playing against the top people in the world you get on the wrong side of the momentum and you just get beaten. But the important thing is to stay in touch and wait for things to start turning your way. That's what happened.'

How much of McGinley's reading of events is true is open to suggestion. It is one plausible answer among many. What is clear is that it has become the most popular version of the story, and proves something that is central to the captain myth, which is that sports fans, the media and the participants want to tell a good story more than we want to tell the truth. When we recall great sporting events we play down one reading of events in place of another more memorable version, allowing minor details to slip so events fit the narrative. In this respect so called 'factual storytelling' such as sports reporting often resembles the work of a Hollywood screenwriter.

Why Butch and Sundance Jumped Off a Cliff

You know the plot. Our two heroes are the greatest bank robbers in the West, leaders of the notorious Hole in the Wall Gang. When the banks up their security, the gang move on to robbing trains. But they do over the same train twice, blowing up a safe by putting too much explosive under it. The railway's owner – E. H. Harriman – gets together the meanest lawmen in America to form a superposse and sends them out to catch and kill Butch Cassidy and the Sundance Kid.

All of the above is true. It happened in real life and was the basis for the plot of the film that won William Goldman the Oscar for best screenplay in 1969.

But Goldman had a problem, one that threatened to undermine the whole film: his heroes ran away. For generations of American filmgoers brought up on Westerns, that isn't what heroes do; John Wayne would stand and fight. How could Goldman make the audience pull for Butch and Sundance while still having them run away?

His solution was to create a chase, in which the superposse outthink Butch and Sundance at every turn – 'Who are those guys?' – until they reach what feels like the end of the road, up on a cliff top with a rocky ravine below. In one of the great scenes in cinema history, Butch and Sundance talk it over – 'Would you make a jump like that if you didn't have to?' – and then leap into the unknown, escaping down the rapids to a rousing soundtrack.

The thing is, that last bit never happened, yet it's the scene that anyone who has seen the film always recalls. They remember it because it was gripping drama and was the turning point that made the story work.

The reality was far less dramatic. It's true that Butch, Sundance and Etta, Sundance's girlfriend (played by Katharine Ross in the film), fled to South America when they heard about the superposse. But there was no chase. The pair left the country, so E. H. Harriman stopped paying the lawmen and the group disbanded. The chase and the cliff scene were storytelling solutions created by Goldman, who had to make the audience actually want the heroes to run away: 'I had to make the superposse so all-powerful, so impregnable to defeat, that people sitting out there in the dark would say, "Yes, for chrissakes, go to Bolivia!"'

Goldman's research into the real Butch Cassidy had unearthed parts of a great story. He had engaging characters and a great opening and closing scene. But he was worried about getting from one to the other. 'My terror was this: the middle section was the one that would kill me,' he wrote in *Which Lie Did I Tell?*

The Butch Cassidy problem highlights something we all know, which is that real life only sometimes makes a great story. Life isn't narrative-shaped. Most of the time, the details don't add up, or conflict with each other, and we have great opening scenes that don't go anywhere, or perfect endings but no cliff scene and no superposse to help get us there.

When this happens, we do what William Goldman did and alter reality, tinker with the order of things. A more truthful explanation of Brookline and Medinah would be harder to digest and be a less satisfying story. It would involve inconsistencies that disrupt the flow of the narrative. It would have good bits that don't go anywhere and endings without clear causes. In short, it would lack a cliff scene. Instead, when the 'Miracle at Medinah' is written up, Ian Poulter's birdie charge on Saturday afternoon is often used to mark the point at which the story turned in Europe's favour, when momentum shifted from the red side to the blue.

How Stories Evolve

Anyone who has ever heard a joke being told for the second time knows that stories evolve. They change in the telling. The good bits are worked on and enhanced to get a bigger laugh, while some of the detail gets dropped or replaced with new, better stuff. The result is that good jokes become stronger over time. They are like sharks, evolution's great winners.

Ryder Cup history is full of sharks: great stories that have remained in place for years and sometimes decades, and which are told over and over and over again, sometimes growing and changing in the process. As we've seen, the concession at Birkdale in 1969 is memorable because of how the story was manipulated by Jack Nicklaus. If Tony Jacklin had made the putt – which he always insists he would have done – the score would have been the same and the result a tie. A rare event in Ryder Cup history, but not a defining one. Nicklaus's concession is a story that propels the 1969 match into Ryder Cup folklore, the event's usable past. In the hands of Sam Snead and Eric Brown, the respective captains that day, the story would have been different. It was Nicklaus's gesture that made it more compelling, giving it the edge that future golf fans love to pass on.

Good stories have a shape to them that makes it easier to remember the details. For example, the tale of Brookline has the perfect comeback shape that makes Justin Leonard's remarkable putt on the 17th feel inevitable, the culmination of a great story. Two years previously, the story of Valderrama '97 is less easy to recall because the story has a different shape, and the ending didn't work out as well. America came into the match as big favourites with Tiger Woods, fresh from his first Masters victory, joined in the team by Justin Leonard and Davis Love, as that year's winners of the Open Championship and USPGA Championship respectively. The Americans went behind on days one and two and then came back on the final day. But they didn't win. America's singles rally was every bit as nail-biting as the Miracle at Medinah or the Battle of Brookline in 1999, it was just that the outcome was less satisfactory, and the comeback story is usually passed over in favour of another type of story, which features Seve's idiosyncratic captaincy, which has became the prevailing narrative. Talk of 1997 and people talk of Seve racing in a buggy around the course, barking orders and changing the course to fit his team. Meanwhile Freddie Couples's demolition of Ian Woosnam by 8 and 7 tends to be glossed over, as is debutant Jim Furyk's inspired win over Nick Faldo, the record points scorer on the European team. These individual success stories get in the way of the bigger tale and so are quietly dropped, and players' reputations are collateral damage.

Likewise, compare how history will treat Poulter's birdie spree with that of Rickie Fowler's at Celtic Manor in 2010. Fowler made four birdies in four holes to bring America to the brink of victory on the final day. We don't talk about Fowler in the same way we do Ian Poulter, because Fowler's birdie blitz had no happy ending. Graeme McDowell made a great putt to win the match, and Fowler has to make do with being a bit-part player in a tale of America's heroic failure.

The story of Medinah will be told many times in the years to come. These recollections may alter slightly depending on the teller. Some details may be added for extra excitement. Ian Poulter's eyes will pop even wider as the final birdie goes in on Saturday night and the length of Justin Rose's putt on the 17th may grow as the years pass, despite YouTube's evidence to the contrary. In that future golf club bar it is unlikely that many will tell the story of Ollie's hairdryer.

The Failed Story of Ollie's Hairdryer

Despite his winning smile and charming manner, José María Olazábal has a ferocious temper. Endearingly, this is usually directed at himself. His agent Sergio Gómez recalled his wife berating Olazábal after she had seen him in club-throwing mode. On another occasion Olazábal's temper surfaced at a Ryder Cup press conference in 2008, in which he played a vice-captain's role to Nick Faldo. At the post-match conference the British sportswriter Paul Hayward asked Faldo whether losing would impact his legacy as one of Britain's greatest players. It was a good question, and a fair one. Olazábal saw things differently, and intervened on his captain's behalf, all but threatening Hayward physically.

The incident proved to be useful data when it came to constructing the first draft of Olazábal's captain myth at Medinah. This positioned him as the archetypal Emotional Southern European, a variation on the Passionate Celt.

It was given a further boost on Saturday morning at Medinah, when Graeme McDowell gave an interview to the BBC on the range before play. Europe were trailing after day one and McDowell said that the captain had been very angry at the team meeting the previous evening. 'We were down and got the hairdryer treatment from José María,' said McDowell. 'We had a sense of belief on Saturday.'

Olazábal confirmed later that the Friday evening session was indeed very fiery. 'Well, it's fair to say I didn't expect to lose the afternoon session by four points to zero,' he said. 'I didn't think we were really up to it over the first four holes on Friday, and we seemed to end up behind from the start. For whatever reason the

Americans started more quickly, with a couple of birdies on those first four holes, and we never managed to make a single birdie. When you're facing great players you cannot allow yourself to get behind. Maybe we were not as prepared as we should have been. Either way, that meeting was a little bit, how should we say it? Tough. Let's put it that way,' he said, laughing at the memory.

The response from the players was mixed. 'They are 12 individuals. Some players will take it well. Some will be surprised. Others will be saying, "I'm trying to do my best here, I don't need this kind of conversation." But I felt that I needed to make the point so that we were clear: they needed to be standing on that first tee ready to go full throttle. That's maybe the toughest part of the captaincy. Dealing with different characters, different people; knowing how to approach them. Some need a little bit of care and love. Some others prefer to come back at you straight in your face. There was a little bit of surprise from a few of the players, they perhaps didn't expect this kind of reaction from me.'

By invoking the hairdryer, McDowell was encouraging reporters to compare Olazábal with the most successful football manager of the past quarter century, Sir Alex Ferguson. Ferguson managed Manchester United from 1986 to 2013, a period in which the team dominated English football, winning 13 Premier League titles, two European Champions League finals and many other trophies. The hairdryer is the defining motif of Ferguson's own leadership myth as the hard-as-nails Scot brought up in Govan, the shipbuilding area of Glasgow. Ferguson's success has helped to frame the idea of management in the minds of a generation of fans and sports journalists. Whenever United came back from behind to win, the hairdryer often felt like the cause.

The problem with McDowell's hairdryer reference was that it didn't fit the chronology of events at Medinah: cause and effect were out of whack.

In a perfect world, Olazábal's team talk would have reaped immediate results. The story of Saturday morning would have been a golfing version of Fergie's ferocious half-time team talks: fresh from being given the hairdryer the team slept fitfully and came out fighting, turning the game around, driven by fear at the prospect of returning to the dressing room to face the wrath of the boss.

This didn't happen. If anything, Team Europe played worse in that first session on Saturday morning, post-ferocious team talk, than they had on Friday afternoon. Lee Westwood and Luke Donald suffered a 7 and 6 defeat at the hands of Mickelson and Keegan Bradley, matching the largest losing margin by a European pairing, equalling the caning dished out to Nick Faldo and David Gilford in 1991 and Des Smyth and Ken Brown in 1979. By midday on Saturday America had won three of the four morning matches, with only Poulter and Rose posting a point for the visitors.

There was no way that the Sunday turnaround could be attributed to the Friday night team meeting, so it was discarded in favour of the Poulter-inspired comeback. As a basis for his captain myth, Olazábal's hairdryer didn't work. It was a cause looking for an effect.

Chapter 13

The Strategy Placebo

If the captain is the storyteller, then strategy is his story. More than anything, the job of the captain is to sell the idea, the vision, of how to get to the summit – in this case represented by 14½ points on Sunday evening. Strategy can bolster a team's confidence by giving the impression of direction, breaking three days of almost nonstop golf into a series of more understandable and manageable tasks. The subtext to strategy is that the captain is in control. It's also a lie.

'"Once upon a time" is code for "I'm about to lie to you",' said Neil Gaiman, the author giving a talk about his craft. 'The act of listening to a story is the act of knowing you are being lied to.'

It would be a brave captain who started his team talk with, 'Once upon a time . . .' But he may as well do, because he's making it up or, at best, he's guessing. Like the readers of a fairytale, for the story to be a success, the audience – the team – must be a willing accomplice, in on the conceit.

'The writer is not an all-powerful architect of our reading experience,' wrote Jonathan Gottschall in *The Storytelling Animal*. 'The writer guides the way we imagine but does not determine it . . . A writer lays down words, but they are inert. They need a catalyst to come to life. The catalyst is the reader's imagination.'

In the same way the captain lays down the framework, but it is the players who provide the catalyst that bring it to life. The best leaders, like the best magicians, are a mixture of salesmen and confidence tricksters: their act is a distraction, which the scriptwriter Christopher Nolan explained in his film *The Prestige*: 'Every great magic trick consists of three parts or acts. The first part is called "the Pledge". The magician shows you something ordinary: a deck of cards, a bird or a man. He shows you this object. Perhaps he asks you to inspect it to see if it is indeed real, unaltered, normal. But, of course . . . it probably isn't. The second act is called "the Turn". The magician takes the ordinary something and makes it do something extraordinary. Now you're looking for the secret . . . but you won't find it because, of course, you're not really looking. You don't really want to know. You want to be fooled. But you wouldn't clap yet. Because making something disappear isn't enough; you have to bring it back. That's why every magic trick has a third act, the hardest part, the part we call "the Prestige".'

Like the captain's strategy, 'the Prestige' is the part of the story we use to explain what we've just seen. 'Our mind is strongly biased towards causal explanations and does not deal well with mere statistics,' wrote Nobel Prize-winning psychologist Daniel Kahneman in his classic book *Thinking, Fast and Slow*, which established just how much we are suckers for a story. Kahneman explains away variations in performance using the statistical phenomenon called 'regression to the mean'. This tells us that extreme scores tend to become less extreme over time; what goes up must come down. The teams' performances at the Ryder Cup are difficult to predict; the results themselves are often unpredictable. When one team takes an early lead this encourages the opposing captain to alter his strategy accordingly. Like the magician's Prestige the captain's strategy is what takes our attention. If the match changes direction, the strategy can look a lot like the cause.

For example, when Davis Love rested Mickelson and Keegan Bradley on Saturday at Medinah it felt, in retrospect, that this was the moment America lost momentum and gave Ian Poulter the opportunity to score five birdies and turn the game Europe's way. Because the players on both teams are so close in terms of ability, often 18 holes is not enough time for the regression to the mean to happen and the match ends before the swing back to the mean is possible. This leaves one player to take the glory and the other to take the hit. 'Causal explanations will be evoked when regression is detected, but they will be wrong because the truth is that regression to the mean has an explanation but does not have a cause.'

'The Strategy Placebo' was at work on Saturday night at the Belfry in 2002. The teams were level 8–8 after the first two days and the captains Sam Torrance and Curtis Strange revealed their line-ups for the Sunday singles matches the next day. With Brookline apparently still fresh in his mind, Torrance front-loaded his order, with Colin Montgomerie out first, followed by García, Clarke, Langer, Harrington and Thomas Bjørn. By contrast, Strange's line-up was notable for his positioning of Tiger Woods and Phil Mickelson, at that point the world's number one and two respectively. The captain put them out at the bottom of the card, with Woods at last place and Mickelson at number 11.

At that Saturday evening press conference, Strange played fake dumb. 'Sam told us he's intentionally front-end loaded, because—' said an American reporter, who was then cut off in mid-sentence by Strange. 'You think? This isn't out of a hat?'

There was a release of laughter around the room at the captain's sarcasm, and the guy with the notebook tried again: 'Sam said he has loaded the front end "because he felt like putting a lot of blue flags up on the board". He thought a lot of blue flags on the board would generate momentum?'

'I know exactly what he's doing,' said Strange, now taking the question seriously.

'You've back-loaded the line-up. What is it exactly you are doing?' asked the reporter, emboldened.

Strange's answer was informative. 'He [Torrance] wants to get the spectators involved early,' he said. 'He wants to get momentum early and hopefully that will feed over into the back-end of his field, of the players'. Strange revealed that his preparation included some scenario planning for what might happen going into the Sunday singles. 'I had two formulas for Sunday,' he said, depending on the closeness of the matches. If the two teams were close going into Sunday, said Strange, he envisaged his line-up would include the following: 'A couple of good, solid players up front – well, two of my horses up front, maybe three'. To balance this line-up, Strange said he would like to see a proven match-winner going out in the latter places to help secure the Cup under the intense pressure of the final holes. This job he gave to Tiger Woods, a decision that was to come back to haunt him. 'And then coming in if it's on the line you certainly have to have a couple of horses down there and certainly it was talked about – I'll be honest with you, it was talked about Tiger not even going last. But if the Ryder Cup is on the line, for any team, that's the guy you have to have go last. So he's last, he's number 12.'

Strange's decision to put Tiger Woods out last was influenced by Dave Marr's handling of Jack Nicklaus in 1981 at Walton Heath, when America brought over arguably its greatest ever team, containing 11 Major champions. 'I had this thing,' says Strange. 'I knew that Dave Marr put Jack [Nicklaus] last. I don't know if Arnold ever played last, but I think he did. I knew that my team needed strength at the end.'

The Virginia-born player was one of the most successful American golfers of the 1980s. In 1988 he became the first man to win $1 million in a single season on the PGA Tour, capping four victories with the first of two back-to-back US Open Championship wins. He played in the Ryder Cup five times from 1983 through to 1995, watching at first hand the transformation of the event as a competitive spectacle. For most of his Ryder Cup career, Strange himself was viewed as the hard man who captains wanted at the end just in case things got close. Jack Nicklaus put Strange last in 1985 and in the bottom three again in 1987. Raymond Floyd sent him out at 12 in 1989, when the player's 2-up victory over Ian Woosnam was critical in a tied match.

Much of the appeal of matchplay golf and of the Ryder Cup in particular, is the do-or-die element, the zero sum game of it's him or me. The heightened pressure in the final holes of a Ryder Cup has few parallels. It is made more intense when a player has a short putt to win the Cup. In large part, the pressure comes from the player's own knowledge that he really should get the ball in the hole. These are the putts they practise for. Stand next to the putting green at a tournament and you'll see players holing hundreds of such putts. A similar psychological game is played when a footballer takes a penalty kick. In his book *On Penalties*, the journalist Andrew Anthony wrote that 'the appeal of the penalty lies ostensibly in its orchestrated suspense. We know something is going to happen but we don't know what it will be'.

This 'orchestrated suspense' is there for all to see in the final throes of a Ryder Cup and the all or nothing penalty shoot-out is a pared down version of the Sunday singles. Similarly, much emphasis is placed on the order in which the key men will line up. At the 2012 European Championships, Portugal played Spain in a semi-final match in Donetsk, Ukraine. The role of Tiger Woods was taken by Portugal's captain and best player, Cristiano Ronaldo, who had entered the competition after a fantastic season with Real Madrid, winners of La Liga, the domestic Spanish league, thanks in large part to the player's incredible 60-goal haul.

Curtis Strange's footballing equivalent was Portugal's team manager Paulo Bento. A conversation between Bento and Ronaldo led to the decision that the captain would wait to take what they assumed would be the all-important fifth and final penalty. But just as Woods was denied the chance to contribute his point, so Portugal had lost the penalty shoot-out before the best player got a chance to score. Two of Ronaldo's teammates missed their spot kicks and the match was sealed by Spain's fourth penalty taker, Cesc Fabregas, leaving Ronaldo standing alone on the halfway line as the Spanish team celebrated a famous victory. Ronaldo told reporters after the match, 'It was just a question of me speaking with the coach. He said to me: "Do you want to take the fifth one?" and I said "yes".

'Sometimes I take the first, the second or the third. I agreed to take the fifth.'

Bento, when asked why Ronaldo did not step up earlier, gave an answer that Curtis Strange could appreciate: 'We had this plan and if it would have been 4-4 and he would taken the last penalty we would be talking in a different way,' he explained. In essence, said Bento, it would be great to have 20/20 hindsight, whereas the media's analysis of the decision put Ronaldo in the frame for grandstanding. He wanted to be the hero, said the Portuguese press, the big man who was there at the end to take the credit; Ronaldo's hubris cost Portugal its place in the final.

When Europe won by 15½ to 12½ at the Belfry in 2002, Curtis Strange's Bad Captain story was set in motion as the man who got his strategy wrong and paid the price.

In one of the biggest surprises in the event's long history, world number two Phil Mickelson lost to Phillip Price, a journeyman from Pontypridd in South Wales who, at the time of the match, was ranked 119th in the world. Price had qualified in the final spot, courtesy of victory in the 2001 Algarve Open de Portugal, only his second ever win on Tour. However, the 2001 Cup was postponed after the terrorist attacks of September 11 and played a year later, in September 2002. By then, Price's form had slipped to the degree that some uncharitable sources were calling for the player to be replaced by someone in better nick. 'Fuck that,' says Torrance today. 'He's earned his way in, there was no way we were going take it away from him.'

Price beat Mickelson 3 and 2 with a 25-foot putt on the 16th hole to claim his place in history. That sort of thing happens in sport, it's why we watch. What happened next, however, defined Curtis Strange's captaincy.

Without Mickelson's expected point, Paul McGinley finished the match with a putt across the 18th green to beat Jim Furyk. This meant that world number one Tiger Woods's match against Jesper Parnevik didn't count, as the game was over before it had reached a conclusion. Strange's singles order exposed him to a particularly virulent post-mortem from the press. The American captain, wrote *Sports Illustrated*'s Rick Reilly, 'handed more gifts to Europe than the Marshall Plan'.

The captain's own defence was that America lost to a team in better form. 'We got beat,' Strange said. 'The score on Sunday was 28–under [for the Europeans] to 8–under [US team]. The facts ruin the stories a lot of times, so the facts never get in there.'

One question Strange gets asked a lot is whether he would do things differently on that Sunday in 2002. He laughs. 'Not really. But I do find it odd when people ask whether I'd do it again – i.e. whether I'd put Tiger out last again. Hell no, we lost. Of course I wouldn't do it again, that would be stupid, wouldn't it?

'When I was named captain I bought a whiteboard and a Sharpie pen and put the whiteboard up in my office. When the team was announced I put the pairings on the whiteboard. On the first day of the event the pairings were identical. I'm just saying that you can overthink these things. I prefer to go by instinct. You've played your whole life by instinct and feel. You know these players – I was somewhat the same age – you know how they play and their personalities. Those sorts of things don't change. The personalities don't change. The way they play doesn't change. I didn't think about the singles line-up until Saturday.'

When he became captain, Strange arranged to speak to every living former American captain. 'I had a ball doing it,' he says today. 'I couldn't get Billy Casper off the phone for an hour.

Byron Nelson and Sam Snead were still around, so I spoke with both of them.' He recalled approaching Jack Nicklaus. 'I was on the course, walking the fairway with Jack. I say to him, "You got anything for me?" He says [Strange does a great Nicklaus impression], "Nah, throw up 12 balls, the two that land closest together can go play." That's how he felt about it. These guys are grown men, treat them like that. Screw the personality differences. I didn't get into that. You got to put that aside. He told me that whatever you do it's OK.'

Compared to Strange, his counterpart Torrance is credited with gaining the upper hand on Sunday by his canny manipulation of momentum, building an irrepressible force in favour of the Europeans. There wasn't much science to it, he says. 'Four or five years after the Ryder Cup I was rooting around in my desk and I found the original order of play for the Sunday singles for the postponed 2001 match. It was exactly the same, man for man, as I put out in 2002.' He recalls the moment he thought of putting out Monty at number one on Sunday. 'It was in 2000, I was sitting next to a member at Sunningdale, Bugsy Holland, a lovely man. He said, "You know, Sam, you could do a lot worse than put your best player out first and your worst player out last."

'I thought about it so many times, every scenario I tried, I couldn't fault it,' said Torrance. 'The other side of the coin was that I would be leaving my rookies to battle it out at the end. I had four rookies in the last five matches. It didn't bother me in the slightest. In that cauldron, when you are going down to the wire in the Ryder Cup, you have to stand up and be counted, or you can fold like a cheap suit. It doesn't matter who you are, and I've seen some fantastic players crack under the pressure. When eight matches were out on the course we were up in seven of them. That's momentum. It didn't mean we were going to win, but that was the start we were looking for.'

Torrance's retelling of events has become the standard official history. However, a more challenging version of what we saw in 2002 was later presented by Professor William Hurley, who combined his love of golf with his expertise in probability and decision analysis to ask a good question: was Curtis Strange wrong or unlucky?

Hurley is Professor of the Royal Military College of Canada and a low single figure handicap golfer, and so studied the decisions of Curtis Strange with more than a casual fan's interest. He watched on as the American captain was given the type of rough treatment by the media that is traditionally the fate of the Bad Captain. In particular, he noted the questions surrounding Strange's placement of Tiger Woods at number 12. Again, the *New York Times* led the way: 'There is no way the Cup should have been settled before Woods could even finish his match. Win or lose, the world's best player should play in a match that matters. Instead, the Europeans were drinking champagne while Woods was on the 18th fairway, in the process of halving a meaningless match against Jesper Parnevik. It would have been one thing to put Woods in the final match if the Americans had been protecting a lead. But with the score tied, 8–8, heading into the singles, the Americans, especially on the road, needed Woods on the course sooner.'

Professor Hurley went about applying some probability theory to the issue. The result was an academic paper called 'The 2002 Ryder Cup: Was Strange's Decision to Put Tiger Woods in the Anchor Match a Good One?' Strange wanted his best players, Mickelson and Woods, playing when the Ryder Cup was most likely to be on the line, and so summarised the three basic arguments:

Argument 1: if your first five to six players play well and win their matches, there will be a 'momentum' effect and it will be easier for the remaining players to win their matches.

Argument 2: if you schedule Woods in the anchor match the Ryder Cup may be over before he has a chance to weigh in.

Argument 3: if you schedule Woods in the anchor match you give yourself the best chance that he plays the decisive match, the match that determines the Ryder Cup.

The first two arguments suggest that Woods should have been scheduled in one of the earlier matches. The last suggests that he should have been played in the anchor match. So where, according to Hurley's number crunching, should Strange have scheduled Woods? At the front end or later in the day, as he actually did?

His answer was that Strange's strategy to put Mickelson out at 11 and Woods at 12 was not only 'defensible, but optimal' – a counterintuitive conclusion that Professor Hurley was happy to explain.

Argument 1: the momentum argument.

Hurley dismissed the momentum story using the work of Daniel Kahneman and Amos Tversky's 'the law of small numbers', which suggests that humans are quick to find a pattern in a random sequence where there isn't one, especially when the sequence is relatively short. 'In both the 1999 and 2002 Ryder Cups,' wrote Hurley, 'one team won the lion's share of the initial singles matches. In 1999, the US won the first six matches; in 2002 the Europeans won 4½ points in the first six matches.

Thereafter, neither the US in 1999 nor the Europeans in 2002 were able to sustain that momentum. In both years each team was only able to win 2½ points in the remaining six matches. This is hardly evidence of momentum given any reasonable statistical interpretation of that word. What it is, quite simply, is a good start.'

Argument 2: the match will be over before Woods can contribute.

In the absence of a momentum effect, thought Hurley, 'it's hard to see how matches could be dependent'. An 'independent' outcome is one that is stationary and is not influenced by other results. For example, Colin Montgomerie's victory over Scott Hoch in match one did not impact on Sergio García winning or losing against David Toms. As an operations researcher, says Hurley, 'one of my built-in biases is that I have absolutely no hesitation in assuming that random variables making up a sequence are independent and stationary'. This he says is 'not such a bad assumption in the context of the Sunday afternoon of a Ryder Cup'. Again, Hurley comes out for Strange.

Argument 3: Strange wanted Woods in the match that was most likely to be the decider.

There is no doubt, says Hurley, that most US team captains would want Woods to be playing the decisive match, all other things being equal (this is a contentious statement given Woods's record in the Ryder Cup, which is poor when set against his performances in tournament golf over the course of his career). The difficulty is that you don't know which match this will be. However, in the position Strange found himself in, needing 6½ points to win, he gave himself the best chance for Woods to play in the decisive match by putting him out at number 12. An alternative thought experiment proves his point, says Hurley. Suppose that Woods is in the anchor match and that the decisive match is match ten, one the US loses before Woods finishes his match. Move Woods to match ten and put the American who lost match ten (Furyk) in the anchor match. Assuming the results of the matches are unaffected by this switch, the Americans still lose the Cup, says Hurley.

'I get the argument that the match was over before we got to Tiger and so he didn't count,' says Strange. 'But it's one of 12 matches, no matter when they go off in the afternoon. They all count. If he had won his match we'd still have lost. It's just that the match was decided before his point was on the board. So I understand the argument but I think it's irrelevant. Maybe I'm subconsciously making excuses, but I don't think so.'

Paul Azinger was the only winning American captain in the first decade of the new millennium. His team for Valhalla in 2008 didn't include Woods, who was absent injured, but he recalls being asked by Fred Couples as to how to handle Tiger in the run-up to a Presidents Cup. 'I told him that the most common mistake captains make is that everybody sends Tiger out first,' said Azinger. 'It makes it too easy to find Tiger Woods. When we played Europe there were players we tried to find. We wanted to find Seve because he was going to be the best and most difficult player and it was easy to find him because he always went off first. Tiger is a guy you target because he's a superstar. If you can identify and practise for the guy who's playing the best, all you have to do is send them out first and you get Tiger Woods. Don't put him out first, and never put him out last. I want his point to count on Sunday. The matches can be decided before you get to the 12th spot. Anyone who has made it onto the team can perform in that 12th spot. It's suffocating pressure but if you put your best player back there and his point doesn't matter I think you've made a huge mistake.'

More than any one single factor, the experience of Curtis Strange in 2002 highlights the issue of luck in deciding the fate of the captain. Luck is a frustratingly bland explanation. It leaves us feeling deflated at the failure of the story to make more sense. The truth, as suggested by William Hurley's analysis, is that we can't always know for sure why some teams win and others lose, despite the miles of newsprint devoted to the subject. This needn't be such a downer, however. Safe in the knowledge that he doesn't have all the answers, a Good Captain will seek to deal in probabilities, seeking to improve the odds of his team by using insight and experience that has been tested time and again in the heat of competition. The alternative is a mirage.

Chapter 14

What Do We Do With a Problem Like Tiger?

Curtis Strange faced a question that has confronted every American captain since 1997: what do I do with Tiger Woods?

The first time most people saw Tiger was in a Nike commercial. 'Hello world,' he said in 1996, a month after signing the first of several enormous endorsement deals. We listened as Woods talked over stirring images of himself as a child, through footage of him as a world-beating amateur. The myth-making iconography remained pretty much in place over the course of nearly two decades; the component parts of Brand Tiger: the fist pump, the smile and the impassive, unrelenting stare into the camera.

Woods captured the imagination in a way no golfer had since Arnold Palmer in the early days of television. The first Major win at Augusta in 1997 was not only brilliant, it was so 'on brand'. The black kid winning at the Masters, where his skin colour would have prevented him playing until 1975 and where it was compulsory to have a black caddie until 1983.

The Tiger of the Nike ads conflicted with the other public version of Tiger Woods, which could be found at press conferences and in media interviews – an environment every bit as false as advertising. Tiger is famously hard to fathom at these moments when he is contractually obliged to talk the media. He is cool, aloof and can sometimes come across as irritated and arrogant. Despite this, the press gave him a remarkably easy ride, either too in awe of the brand or too scared of his handlers to delve too deep or ask difficult questions. In this way Tiger's relationship with the media pre-2008 was somewhat out of time, a throwback to the way Hollywood curated their stars' images during its 'golden era' of the 1930s, when famous people were untouchable, protected by the film studios' publicity machines. Few of us peered too far behind the billboard façade that had been erected for our enjoyment. When the billboard version of Tiger fell over in 2008, the real Tiger was there for all to see and, like most of us, it wasn't pretty. Unlike the flawless face on the poster, the real one had warts. In other words, he was human, and we hated him for it.

Both versions of Tiger – the man and the brand – have been a fascinating side story to the Ryder Cup since he made his debut at Valderrama in Tom Kite's team. He travelled to Spain as the holder of the Masters green jacket, but his form was frustratingly sketchy. This was put down to first-night nerves, or tiredness, or trying too hard to be the boy wonder, as one caddie put it. The deeper analysis into Woods's erratic relationship with the event would come later.

Kite partnered Woods with his friend Mark O'Meara on the first morning of the match. Expectations were oddly low even then, this time due to the course, which Ballesteros had tricked up to favour the home team. 'If you are going to pick a course in the whole world that would be a bad course for Tiger Woods, this is it,' said Johnny Miller. 'It is the narrowest course and has the smallest greens I've ever seen. It's got trees overhanging the fairways. This is a precision course. This is a Ben Hogan course . . . it is not a Tiger Woods course.'

Despite Miller's concerns, Woods settled well enough. He hit a 2-iron from the tee of the 535-yard fourth followed by a 9-iron lay-up and a wedge to the green, holing the putt for a perfectly executed 'Hogan-like' birdie. This gave the partnership a lead over Montgomerie and Langer they would never relinquish, running out 4 and 2 winners on the 16th.

The good start was misleading. The same four players went out against each other in the afternoon, with the European pair handing out a 5 and 3 win. Woods went from OK to worse the next day when he blew the last hole of the fourball, again partnered with O'Meara. In front of former President George Bush, Woods putted off the 18th green into water, finally going down 2 and 1 to Faldo and Westwood. Worse was to come for Tiger on Sunday, when he went down 4 and 2 to the unfancied Italian Costantino Rocca, leaving the American with a 1–3–1 record for his first three days in Team USA colours.

The up and down nature of that first outing has been repeated many times since. In a career that has had many high points, it's unlikely that he has ever played better than he did through 1999 and 2000, either side of Brookline. Woods won eight times on the PGA Tour in 1999, the first player to achieve this feat since Nicklaus in 1974. A few weeks before the Ryder Cup, he had seen off the challenge of Sergio García to take the USPGA

Championship, the final Major of the year. The season that followed was even better. In 2000, Woods won six consecutive Tour events, the longest winning streak since Byron Nelson in 1948, and he became the youngest player ever to win all four Major championships, broke the scoring record for the lowest stroke average in tour history and won three of that year's Majors, including the US Open, by ten shots. Not for the last time, however, Woods failed to bring this level of play to the Ryder Cup. Ben Crenshaw paired him with three different partners during the week – Tom Lehman, David Duval and Steve Pate – and got just half a point from a possible four in return over the first two days.

'You kind of scratch your head and say, "What do I do to help this guy?"' wrote Crenshaw later.

The pattern was set, as subsequent captains tried and largely failed to find a formula that would bring the real Tiger Woods to light in American colours. Across Ryder and Presidents Cups, Woods has had 18 different playing partners since he teed off with O'Meara at Valderrama. In addition, Woods is 9–3–2 in his singles matches across his 14 Ryder and Presidents Cups and 33–31–4 in matches at these competitions.

The numbers only tell part of the story. Since the 2004 Cup at Oakland Hills, the apparently toxic relationship between Woods and Phil Mickelson has become a Ryder Cup case study in what can go wrong when pairing players for the first two days of the competition.

Captain Hal Sutton put the two players out together for the first two matches on Friday, both of which they lost. Sutton was pilloried for the decision that came to define his captaincy. Yet Sutton's strategy of pairing Woods and Mickelson was seen as a bold and innovative strategy in some quarters. Before the match there was talk of a potential masterstroke, not least from the players themselves.

'You've seen Watson and Nicklaus go at it and they have won matches; Nicklaus and Palmer in the Ryder Cup together,' said Tiger before the match began. 'It can be perceived as both ways. But I think if [Phil and I] win matches it will be perceived as a huge plus.'

This optimism was undone by events. Woods and Mickelson lost both their games on the first day, albeit by small margins. In the morning fourballs they were beaten 2 and 1 by Colin Montgomerie and Pádraig Harrington, who combined brilliantly to make a remarkable eight birdies in the first 11 holes.

In the afternoon, the Americans lost by one hole to Lee Westwood and Darren Clarke in the foursomes. Woods and Mickelson took an early lead and were level as the match went down the 18th. Mickelson then hit an awful tee shot that came to rest against an out-of-bounds fence. The alternate shot format meant that Woods was forced to then take a penalty drop and took his next shot from behind a tree some 260 yards from the green. 'It basically cost us the match,' said an apologetic Mickelson.

After the round, Lee Westwood gave a fair assessment of what he'd seen on the 18th tee. 'It's probably an uncomfortable tee shot for Phil,' said Westwood. 'He likes to fade the ball, the hole is sloping the wrong way, the wind is off the left for him. He chose to hit a 3-wood, and everybody is entitled to . . . everybody can make a bad swing every now and again. It's just he did it at a critical time in the match.'

Westwood's analysis was a rare piece of balance in the rush to explain Europe's unprecedented 6½ to 1½ lead after the first day.

Mickelson's tee shot was deemed too significant to be just a random bad swing and has since become emblematic of America's failures. Few golf strokes have been worked harder than Mickelson's tee shot on the 18th at Oakland Hills: this was not just a duff stroke, it was elevated to reflect something rotten at the heart of Team USA.

The reason for this over-analysis was due in part to the fact that Mickelson had switched club manufacturer just before the event, moving from Titleist to Callaway in a deal rumoured to be worth several millions to the player. As his ball sailed out of bounds, the Callaway deal was held up as evidence of Mickelson's greed and selfishness. Why did he take such a risk with his form weeks before the Ryder Cup? Would he have made such a big move weeks before the Masters? Mickelson's preparation for the 2004 Cup is regularly cited as evidence of the way America's best players put self before the team. The player compounded this criticism by declining a Wednesday practice round with Woods, his alternate shot partner. This was the players' usual event preparation but it meant the first time Mickelson hit Woods's Nike ball was when he settled over the second shot in the Friday afternoon foursomes.

The antipathy between the players is often traced to comments made by Mickelson about Woods's Nike equipment in 2003. 'In my mind, Tiger and I don't have issues between us,' Mickelson told *Golf* magazine. 'Well, maybe one. He hates that I can fly it past him now [off the tee]. He has a faster swing speed than I do, but he has inferior equipment. Tiger is the only player who is good enough to overcome the equipment he's stuck with.'

The comment drew a surprisingly vehement response from Nike. The company released a factsheet highlighting what had happened when Phil and Tiger had met on the course over the previous year. It was titled '2002 Tiger Woods and Phil Mickelson, Head-to-Head' and contained the following data:

Number of times Tiger Woods and Phil Mickelson paired in competition = 14

Number of times Tiger Woods finished ahead of Phil Mickelson = 12

Number of Tiger Woods wins = 5

Number of Phil Mickelson wins = 0

What had started as a personal issue between two players was turned into a defence of corporate reputation, which amplified the issue in the media. 'We talked and cleared the air,' said Woods. 'Everything is fine. No worries. As we all know, Phil can try to be a smart alec at times. I think that was one of those instances where it just backfired on him.' Mickelson, for his part, was contrite: 'I did not mean anything malicious by it, and I wasn't trying to make a derogatory statement towards anybody. I still should not have gone in that area.'

Whatever the facts of the relationship between the two players, other factors have been conveniently swept under the carpet in the rush to blame Hal Sutton. A more balanced reporting of the facts would mention that 2004 was not a great year for Woods, which may have affected his play at Oakland Hills. He was working with coach Hank Haney to alter his swing and his record reflected this tumult: he had just one top-ten finish in the Majors in 2004, a tie for ninth place at the British Open. The best player in the world that year was the Fijian Vijay Singh, who replaced Woods at the top of the world rankings.

The famed lack of chemistry between Phil and Tiger doesn't explain their relatively poor overall Ryder Cup records. In his other matches that year Mickelson partnered David Toms for a foursomes win on Saturday afternoon, but was beaten by Sergio García in the singles on Sunday by 3 and 2. Woods won his Saturday fourball match with Chris Riley, but then lost his foursomes with Davis Love 4 and 3, beaten by the Irish pair of Pádraig Harrington and Paul McGinley. The news has not been much better since 2004, despite never again having been paired together. Woods's record remains pedestrian given his standing in the game. He found a regular partner in Steve Stricker, who was given a captain's pick at Medinah mainly to play that role, but the pair lost every match they played, going down 0–3.

Lately, some sportswriters have been revisiting Sutton's 'idiotic notion' of pairing the best two players of their generation together. The gist of the argument is that Tiger and Phil are different players than they were in 2004, and different men. Time's a great healer and all that. 'I thought we gelled,' said Tiger of his relationship with Phil. 'We just didn't make enough putts.'

The received wisdom is that putting Woods and Mickelson together was never going to work because they don't like each other. This may or may not be true, but there have been plenty of examples of players winning together who don't see eye to eye away from the course. Ian Woosnam and Nick Faldo were a successful pairing for Europe in 1987 and 1989, winning 3½ points out of four at Muirfield Village and a further 2½ points at the Belfry. This despite Faldo, by his own admission, being a loner with few friends on Tour, a fact that made the job of finding a good partner more difficult.

'I can see some partnerships come together like ham and eggs – Ballesteros and Olazábal immediately springs to mind – whereas with others there may be a multitude of permutations that might or might not work,' wrote Faldo in his autobiography *Life Swings*. 'What flash of divine inspiration persuaded Tony Jacklin to pair Ian Woosnam, the dedicated party animal, with me at Muirfield Village in 1987? . . . Chalk and cheese me and Woosie might have been off the course, but for two days we operated like a mind-reading double act, the notorious free-spirited Welshman in tandem with the meticulous Englishman, who would not even trim his fingernails during a tournament lest it interfere with his touch.'

This is Faldo's somewhat selective memory of the Woosnam–Faldo combination, which conveniently ignores what happened at the next match, at Kiawah Island in 1991, where they lost twice in a day in the anchor partnership. Having gone unbeaten in their first seven matches together (5–0–2) they had now lost three in a row dating back to the Belfry in 1989.

Having won the Masters earlier that year, Ian Woosnam was world number one, a place ahead of Faldo. 'They had been successful in the last two matches,' Bernard Gallacher said. 'So, along with Seve and Ollie, we had two cast-in-stone partnerships. But Nick and Ian didn't gel, and it wasn't until later I found out they didn't really want to play together. By then they had lost two matches on the first day.'

Gallacher puts forward a theory as to the implosion of the Woosnam–Faldo pairing, suggesting that there is a need for an imbalance in the relative status between the players. When Faldo was obviously top dog, Woosnam was happy to let the Englishman be in charge. By '91, however, with Woosnam officially ranked as the best player in the world, the dynamic between the two men had altered. 'In the past, Woosnam had looked up to Faldo, who made all the decisions,' Gallacher told Bruce Critchley, whereas in 1991 they were competing with each other to be top dog.

Such psychology was not how it was done in the old days. Tony Jacklin recalled the decision made by Dai Rees, who tended to put players together for the week. 'Dai paired me with the Welshman Dave Thomas,' wrote Jacklin. 'Dave could hit the ball absurd distances, but his wedge play and chipping were famously suspect. He and I did the maths and deduced that I should tee off at all the odd holes in the foursomes since the par 5s were all odd holes. This meant that if Dave, in hitting his second shot off my drive, was unable to reach the green, then it would be up to me, with my superior short game, to hit the third shot, thereby sparing Dave from having to do it on holes we'd be expected to birdie. And luckily, all the par 3s were even holes, which meant Dave would hit the ball; again, if he missed the green I'd be there to do the chipping. It all made eminent good sense, the kind of common sense I've seen many a Ryder Cup captain fail to employ in the decades since. Hal Sutton putting Tiger and Phil as partners? Mark James putting our weakest players in the opening spots in the singles line-up at Brookline?'

Chapter 15

A-Pods

President John F. Kennedy created the Navy SEALs in 1962 when it became clear that traditional methods of warfare were not going to apply in the jungles of Vietnam. Since the sixties, the SEALs have become one of the most mythologised and controversial fighting units in the world, heavily involved in the American government's foreign policy interventions overseas, in places such as Grenada, Iraq and Afghanistan. It was a Navy SEAL's top secret 'Team 6' operation that tracked down and shot Osama bin Laden in 2011 and the unit's ruthless approach to combating guerrilla warfare has been lionised by popular culture – from Hollywood blockbuster films such as *Zero Dark Thirty* and *American Sniper* through to the mega-selling computer game franchise *Call of Duty*. The secret of the SEALs success is often attributed to a famously tough 30-month training regime, allowing the unit to boast a drop-out rate approaching 75 per cent, and reinforcing the message that only the toughest survive. A platoon consists of 16 SEALs – two officers, one chief, 13 enlisted men – and every member is qualified in diving, parachuting, and demolition. Underpinning the physical training regime is an equally vigorous approach to teamwork, reinforced by a code of conduct that demands each member sign up to a set of agreed standards of behaviour. These include 'I am never out of the fight', 'I will not fail' and membership of the Navy SEALs 'is a privilege that I must earn every day'.

It takes a particularly lively imagination to make the leap from Vietnam to Valhalla, a suburb of Louisville, Kentucky, but that's what Paul Azinger did in 2008. What's more, he was such a good storyteller he took 12 of America's best golfers with him for the ride.

The type of dominance enjoyed by American teams of the 1960s was replicated by Europe in the first decade of the new millennium. Having won at the Belfry in 2002, Europe didn't just beat America in 2004 and 2006, they humiliated them.

'Let's have no more talk about the Americans having the best players, the most Major championships, the strongest team. They are now the underdogs in this every-other-year match-up, unable to compete with the camaraderie, creativity, or fearlessness of their European counterparts.' That's the report from Associated Press the morning after Tom Lehman's team had been dismantled in Ireland in 2006.

The job of the 2008 captain, which the PGA of America gave to Azinger, was to stop the bleeding. Azinger had enjoyed a successful and long career after entering the PGA Tour in 1982. He won 12 times, including the 1993 PGA Championship. But it was his Ryder Cup appearances that helped define him as a feisty competitor who thrived in the unique atmosphere of matchplay golf. He played on four US Ryder Cup teams, an experience that he felt gave him an insight into why Team Europe were so successful: 'Seve and Ollie played together, the Irish stick together, and the Swedes. This is how they have always done it. If they had paired on the basis of technical strengths, they would have put Seve and Langer together, which would have been, on paper, a very strong pairing – but I doubt it would have worked in the same way as it did with Ollie, just because of the personal chemistry between the Spanish guys.'

The title of his book about Valhalla was *Cracking the Code*, an attempt to capture what he had always felt was the difference between the two teams: 'I just felt that the code that Europe has, the intangible advantage they have over us, lay in the way their team was formed. The Spaniards are bonded together by blood. The Swedes play together, the Irishmen, the Scots. When there is a cross over national boundaries it is Lee Westwood and Darren Clarke, and they are best friends. Europe has small groups naturally in place within the team.'

He compared the European group dynamic at the Ryder Cup with that of the international team that competes in the Presidents Cup (a similar team event in which America has been noticeably more successful). At the Presidents Cup, says Azinger, America seem to play as more of a cohesive unit – they become 'the smaller place' when set against 'this giant group from Canada, South Africa, South Korea, Fiji and Australia'. Given the geographical disparity of the international team, he says, 'How can they expect to have the same bond as the Europeans?'

Azinger's pod story took the Ryder Cup captaincy into uncharted waters. It combined the language of the leadership industry with quasi-military team-building techniques, focused on six elements:

1) Break the 12-man team into small pods of four players each

2) Place players in pods based on their personality types rather than on particular strengths in their golf games

3) Change the traditional Ryder Cup points system to allow 'hotter' players to win a place on the team. Also, give the captain four 'captain's picks' instead of two

4) Control the controllables

5) Trust and empower assistant coaches and players

6) Communicate with each golfer appropriately, based on his personality type

Each pod was given a name and allocated a vice-captain.

The Aggressive Pod: defined by Azinger as 'guys who believed they could take charge of situations and pursue a systematic approach to solve problems'. This pod was filled by Phil Mickelson, Anthony Kim, Hunter Mahan and Justin Leonard.

The Influential Pod: this group was defined as 'guys who generated enthusiasm and are comfortable interacting with others'. The players making up this group were Kenny Perry, Jim Furyk, J. B. Holmes and Boo Weekley.

The Steady Eddies: 'These would be the unflappable guys, the ones who wouldn't get too high or low.' Into this pod were put Stewart Cink, Steve Stricker, Ben Curtis and Chad Campbell.

'Barring injury or illness, I will never take you out of your pod,' Azinger told his team at the start of the week. 'I want you to strategise together, prepare together, and I want you to sell out completely for the guys in your small group.' Such was his faith in his system, Azinger put it at the centre of all the major captaincy decisions, including the team order, the partnerships, even the selection of wildcards – Steve Stricker, Chad Campbell, J. B. Holmes and Boo Weekley – who were chosen from a shortlist given to the players who had already played their way onto the team.

More than anything else, Azinger's big idea was a triumph of salesmanship. Getting the players to buy into his system was the difference between it working and not, between Azinger joining the leadership industry or becoming a joke told in team-building seminars, placed in the stocks next to Hal Sutton or Curtis Strange for the crime of making high-profile decisions that went against them.

Storytelling was, says Azinger, a key part of his leadership toolkit: 'My strength as a captain was that I had an idea and was influential enough as a personality to get them to buy in. And to a man they were sold out for this concept. I was strong enough to talk them into believing that this was the right approach. It's true that leaders are storytellers and there is a motivational aspect to this.'

Stories, however, can only get you so far.

It Helps if You Can Fight

Dow Finsterwald was a veteran of four consecutive American Ryder Cup teams of the late 1950s and 1960s, and captained the team in 1977. Finsterwald tells a story about a boxer he'd seen making the sign of the cross while kneeling in his corner, a habit he repeated before every bout. The boxer won regularly, prompting someone to ask him whether he thought praying did any good. 'Yes, sir,' said the boxer, 'but it also helps if you can fight.'

It was a story that talked to Azinger. You can tell a great leadership story, but if the players aren't up to it, you'll lose.

His big idea was dead in the water unless America could get its best team to Valhalla. This proved harder than it looked. Azinger, like Jack Nicklaus before him, didn't trust the world rankings and the money lists to reward the type of player that thrived in man-on-man matchplay golf. He wanted proven winners, not 'walking ATMs' who went from tournament to tournament accumulating cash rather than trophies and green jackets.

Azinger set about lobbying the petty bureaucrats of the PGA of America to get them to change the rules that governed how players qualified for Team USA. He wanted three changes, all of which were politically difficult. Azinger wanted to limit the time period for qualifying to one year instead of two; base the qualifying on money earned rather than top-ten finishes and, thirdly, he wanted four picks instead of two. The latter had been introduced in 1989 following back-to-back defeats in the mid-1980s. Before then, a first-past-the-post system had been used, whereby the leading 12 Americans on the PGA Tour money list at the end of the season were automatically on the team.

This was a throwback to the days of old, when the PGA Tour was dominated by Americans, and only a small handful of foreigners were playing in America – men such as Gary Player, Tony Jacklin, Kel Nagle and Bob Charles. In 2008, the number of foreigners on the American Tour had mushroomed to include many of the Europeans who would line up against Azinger's team at Valhalla. Under the qualifying system Azinger inherited, players earned points for a win and more points in the Major championships. These points doubled in the year of the Ryder Cup. Azinger worried that this sent the wrong message to players trying to make the team.

'I only choked for two things,' Azinger wrote. 'Cash and prestige.' With this in mind he insisted that incentives were changed to reflect this reality: reward the elements of the game that determine what makes a winner, and don't reward mediocrity; in this case awarding points for the players who rarely competed but made piles of cash by finishing down the field.

The most politically contentious change was to load the second year of the two-year qualification period. This was aimed at identifying the players who would likely be most in form – or 'hot' – in the year when the Ryder Cup was going to take place. What this meant in practice was that only points scored at the four Major championships of the first year – the Masters, the Open Championship, the US Open and the USPGA Championship – would count.

This was a big call. By taking all the PGA Tour events out of the first year of qualifying, it lowered the profile of the Tour in favour of the Majors. This pushed a fingernail down the faultline that runs through American golf between the PGA of America, which owns and organises the Ryder Cup, and the PGA Tour, which controls the tournament schedule in the US, outside of the Major championships.

Along with the structural changes in the selection process, Azinger was keen that his team prepared for the match in the same way they did for regular Tour events or Major championships. 'There is no shortcut, you can't hope for it or wish for it, but you have to prepare. At a certain point, as the captain, you have to get out of the way. These are the hottest players we have to offer. The advantage I had was that we had won just three times in 25 years, and lost three of the previous four matches since our miracle comeback in 1999 [at Brookline]. We could have lost four or five matches going into my match.'

Azinger put his 'aggressive pod' out first in the Friday morning foursomes, pitching Mickelson and Kim against the European pair Pádraig Harrington – who had won the USPGA Championship two weeks previously – and the Swedish player Robert Karlsson, that year's leading money winner on the European Tour. The match was halved, but the second half of the pod came good in the second match, when Leonard and Mahan beat Henrik Stenson and Paul Casey 3 and 2 to claim the first point. This gave America a lead they never relinquished over the course of the three days of competition.

Three of his four wildcard picks played a central role – only Steve Stricker struggled to justify his inclusion. Hunter Mahan played all five games and scored 3½ points, while J. B. Holmes and Chad Campbell both won two matches out of three, including important singles victories over Søren Hansen and Pádraig Harrington respectively.

The American captain was true to his word and the pods were kept together throughout the matches. 'Stewart Cink said it was a really weird Ryder Cup,' said Azinger, 'because he didn't see another player hit a shot, apart from the other guys in his pod, until the matches were over and we followed the guys coming in on Sunday.'

On Sunday afternoon, Azinger's pods had won the match at Valhalla by a convincing five-point margin, their first victory, home or away, since Brookline in 1999.

A Question of Authenticity

Winning solves everything. Yet there was a problem with Azinger's pod plan, which he readily acknowledges and which would doubtless have arisen in his Bad Captain story had he lost in 2008. The crux of the strategy was to place players in pods 'based on their personality types rather than on particular strengths in their golf games'. How could Azinger achieve this with any degree of accuracy? Without some attempt at a psychological profile of every player, the Navy SEALs analogy is dead in the water.

The degree to which the SEALs focus on psychology was revealed in a piece of research carried out at the Naval Health Research Centre, the details of which were declassified by the American government in 1994. The primary objective of the study was to collect baseline demographic and personality data on SEALs that could then be used to improve selection and training. The SEALs conduct highly specialised missions in the harshest conditions, requiring significant financial investment in training. If they could select people better they could reduce the drop-out rate and save money.

The research collected data from 139 SEAL personnel aged between 20 and 45 who were stationed in varying bases across the

States. The personalities of the SEALs were categorised under five headings: neuroticism, extraversion, openness, agreeableness and conscientiousness. The results were collected after exhaustive testing over a period of months to find the personality make-up of the 'average SEAL'. Even given this extensive research the Navy still face the problem of interpretation of the data. For example, the average Navy SEAL scores higher than the average American in the five tested categories, but is this cause or correlation? Does the fierce SEAL training regime create people with higher than average scores, or is it due to self-selection, as people with high scores are the ones more likely to want to test themselves by joining the SEALs in the first place?

Azinger didn't have the time, resources or the right to profile his players to anywhere near the veracity carried out by the SEALs. But he knew some of the team well, men he had played with on Tour and in previous Ryder and Presidents Cups – men such as Phil Mickelson, Jim Furyk, Stewart Cink and Steve Stricker. Others, however, he barely knew at all, particularly younger players such as Anthony Kim, J. B. Holmes and Boo Weekley, for example. Without some 'science' behind his psychological profiles, the pods would lack authenticity and be revealed as just a story with no substance. So he had to fudge.

A Reliable Enough Pairing

Isabel Briggs Myers and her mother Katharine Cook Briggs created a system in America in the 1940s based on the work of the famous psychologist Carl Jung. The initial intention was to produce a test that allowed women to find suitable jobs to aid the war effort. It has since been adopted by many companies as a way of aiding the recruitment of staff and in team building, to the extent that more than two million people are thought to take the test each year in America alone. The test is usually conducted through a very detailed questionnaire which attempts to identify respondents by one of 16 possible personality types. These include whether someone is an extrovert or introvert, if they make decisions using their senses or their intuition, if they prefer structure and order compared to flexibility and openness, and so on. This information is processed by the test, and each respondent is given a score, which is an approximation of their personality type. There are now many online variations of Myers–Briggs, however human resources professionals advise that the test should be administered by a trained and qualified practitioner who can then follow up the initial results to process them thoroughly.

Working with Dr Ron Braund, a clinical therapist and business advisor, Azinger drew up a list of players who had the potential to play their way onto his team. Braund then used Myers–Briggs to put a personality type against each of those players. 'While observing players on the course at PGA Tour events, I drew upon information from two assessment tools used during my career as a licensed therapist and team builder,' wrote Braund. 'These profiles [using the Myers–Briggs Type Indicator system] helped to identify personality traits and behavioural styles for player compatibility.'

Using the information gathered by Braund's observations, he created a traffic-light system to label partnerships that ranged from compatible to toxic, awarding either a red, yellow or green light.

Despite not being there in person at Valhalla, Tiger Woods's name cropped up during Azinger's initial player meeting when he presented his controversial traffic-light system to the players for the first time. 'We looked at everyone's compatibility based on red-light, caution-light and green-light scenarios,' said Azinger. 'For example, Phil and Tiger would be a definite red light.' Mickelson laughed it off. 'You didn't have to go there, Zinger,' he said, to laughter from the other team members.

Five years on Azinger offered more detail on the controversial traffic-light system. 'We wanted green-light personalities together. We determined that Tiger Woods and Phil Mickelson would be red-light personalities. It doesn't mean they can't win. They should still win. Jack and Arnold were red-light personality types, but they were just so good that they would win. I felt personality types together were more important than guys whose games complement each other. Seve and José María's personalities were a perfect fit. But put Seve with Bernhard Langer, it would have been a complete red light. Seve with David Gilford is a green light, someone who he can be in charge of. Langer's not that type, they become more of a caution or red light together. Doesn't McDowell try to make McIlroy better? He does. Didn't Seve want to make Olazábal better, and vice versa?'

America lost the next three Ryder Cups after Valhalla, a period which just added lustre to Azinger's Good Captain story. The longer America went without winning, the more the pods lingered in the memory of the players, adding pressure on subsequent captains.

There remains a feeling that America missed a trick by not going with Azinger for 2010. His supporters grumble that he could have been a Jacklinesque figure, offering a continuity that America's Ryder Cup effort has lacked since the early 1980s. As the only American captain to win for more than a decade, why wasn't a variation on Azinger's pod system adopted by subsequent captains?

Since Tony Jacklin created the modern Team Europe in the early 1980s, no European captain has dared to stray too far from the status quo. There have been minor adaptations, but the main planks remain in place: the team room, the 'them and us' mentality, the status symbolism of cashmere and first-class travel. Why can't Team USA find the same consistency behind the scenes?

Curtis Strange, a colleague of Azinger's on ESPN, said he was surprised it wasn't discussed more. 'He thinks about things differently, whether it was the whole pod psychological thing or anything else. It would have been interesting to see if it would have worked again. He'd have done it in a second.' A number of the players in Azinger's team have given him a ringing endorsement. Jim Furyk said that it was the first Ryder Cup he'd gone into where he wasn't so obsessed with his own game but more how he could make others better.

The man himself has said that he initially told the PGA of America that he wasn't interested but then changed his mind. 'But by then it was too late,' said Azinger. 'I did lobby for it at the end. I wanted to carry the flag to Europe, but it was the eleventh hour. I don't know how close it was. In my mind I was very much wanting to do it at the very end, but I waited too long.'

Whatever the future holds, Azinger can look back on 2008 with pride. 'We had that magic in '08. Nobody wanted to let anyone in their group down. They didn't see any of the other players in their team until they got to the clubhouse. Europe has somehow found this magic that enables them to play better. And I'm not trying to suggest that they aren't just better players – they might be – but there is also this intangible element at play. And I think I identified it in 2008.'

Chapter 16

Motifs and Counter-Stories

President Obama rose from a broken home to become the first African-American President of the United States. George W. Bush gave up alcohol in favour of Christianity. Nelson Mandela walked from incarceration to lead his people to power. German Chancellor Angela Merkel was born under communism before leading Europe's most capitalist country.

Every major politician has a story we always remember, which helps us define him or her. It has little to do with policy detail but instead speaks to the type of person they are, the values they hold or the challenges they have faced to get where they are. These leadership stories are often true, can sometimes be enhanced a little, or be outright fabrications. They usually describe a period of dramatic change in the person's life, and their effect is to anchor the individual in the public imagination.

In the same way, the art of political storytelling distils complex areas of policy into easily digestible soundbites. This is done using clever, simple statements that are repeated over and over and over again, until they become impossible to forget. Former British Prime Minister Tony Blair realised that the electorate were too busy, or too lazy, to take in the minutiae of complicated issues like school and social policy. Into this knowledge gap, Blairite policy was distilled. 'Education, education, education,' became Blair's mantra, along with, 'Tough on crime, tough on the causes of crime.'

In the cutthroat world of party politics, these positive soundbites and leadership stories face competition from political opponents who try to alter perceptions by spreading counter-stories. For many British voters, former Labour Party leader Ed Miliband will always be the 'man who stabbed his brother David in the back' to become party leader and so further his own political career. British Prime Minister David Cameron often tried to play down his privileged background. The BBC journalist Gavin Esler noted in his book, *Lessons from the Top, How Successful Leaders Tell Stories to Get Ahead – and Stay There*, how Cameron chose to present himself to the public: 'David Cameron tried to defuse the damaging counter-story that he is a posh, wealthy Etonian who joined an ultra-posh Oxford dining club, the Bullingdon, and married into the aristocracy. He does this by constantly reminding us that he is "Dave" Cameron, an ordinary bloke at home in jeans and T-shirts, someone who just happens to be prime minster and a multimillionaire.' Photos of Cameron cycling on the streets of London, notes Esler, are comparatively easy to find on the internet because they tell the right story, of an ecologically aware and emotionally intelligent urbanite. Go look for one of Cameron in the white tails uniform of the Bullingdon Club, and you will be in front of Google for days. Equally, pictures of Cameron on horseback – he is a keen rider – are hard to find. This is because pictures of a rich man riding through the shires of southern England tell the 'wrong' story and have been removed by those who seek to steer the Cameron narrative.

Think of Nick Faldo the player and several positive stories present themselves. A generation of British golf fans recall staying up late on a Sunday night in 1990 to watch him beat Ray Floyd in a play-off for his second Masters win. They recall the image of Faldo standing in the evening murk on the 11th green, putter aloft in celebration. The player's remorseless, brilliant destruction of Greg Norman at the 1996 Masters is another Faldo memory. He shot 67 in the final round to Norman's 76, to claw back a six-shot deficit and take his third green jacket. The great English player had been given a four-year run-in to the captaincy due to a one-off decision by the European Tour to announce two captains together. When Woosnam got the nod for 2006, Faldo was given the job for Valhalla in 2008.

The rationale was sound. Faldo was enjoying a successful second career as a television pundit in America, a job to which he was well suited. His six Major wins and the record number of Ryder Cup points was something few in the commentary box could equal. The CV lends Faldo's views gravitas, a lucrative commodity.

After famously dismantling and rebuilding his own golf swing in the mid-1980s, the Englishman knows far more about the technical aspects of the game than most. The final, and much underestimated, part of his qualification as a TV pundit is that Faldo is rich enough not to care whether his views offend the current crop of players. Tiger Woods, Rory McIlroy and Colin Montgomerie are just three to have been on the receiving end of a Faldo critique. To golf viewers used to soft soap and pulled punches, Faldo is a refreshing breath of fresh air.

'Don't let the bastards grind you down,' said Faldo to Norman as they walked off the 18th together at Augusta in '96. He was talking about the media awaiting Norman in the press room, but it was a comment that for most of his playing career was his own mantra.

This was because Faldo's relationship with the media has always been difficult and, as such, golf journalists have their own set of Faldo counter-stories, which are not nearly as positive and tend not to focus on his golf game. They recall his speech after he won the Open Championship at Muirfield in 1992, when he thanked the media 'from the heart of my bottom' and then sang them an excruciating version of 'My Way'. 'How can we get the blood to drip out onto the paper?' was how Faldo later described the *modus operandi* of the British media in the eighties and nineties. 'Now they want to do lifestyle pieces. Apparently they have changed, which is great for me and for the good of civilisation.'

It's a rare newspaper profile that doesn't reference Faldo as being an only child or mention his teenage love of solitary pursuits like cycling and fishing. Then there are the divorces, the quote from his second wife Gill, who labelled him forever 'socially, a 24-handicapper' and the story of Brenna Cepelak, a 23-year-old girlfriend who smashed up Faldo's Porsche with a 9-iron after their three-year affair ended. ('She was a right piece of work,' said Faldo later.)

His fellow players were another group who found Faldo's 2008 rebrand hard to swallow. His contribution to successive Ryder

Cups was described succinctly by three-time captain Bernard Gallacher. 'What did Faldo bring to the team?' Gallacher was asked in 1995. 'Points,' he replied. '[He] should have been nicer on the way up, something I think he now regrets,' said Colin Montgomerie, whose own brilliant Ryder Cup playing career was effectively ended when Faldo didn't pick him as a wildcard for Valhalla. In a previous Cup, when Monty was to be paired in the alternate shot format with Faldo, the Englishman sent him a box of his own balls for him to practise with. They had 'Nick Faldo' written on the side. In eight appearances between 1991 and 2006, Montgomerie had been a colossus for Team Europe, winning 23½ points, leaving him just 1½ points shy of overcoming Faldo's record of 25 career points, the most ever won by a European. When the time came for Faldo to inform Monty that he wasn't in his team, the Scot deserved more than the voice message he received from the captain.

Faldo's backstory and his fragile relationship with players and the media meant that there was plenty of material stocked away should a Bad Captain narrative be required after Valhalla. In April 2008, American captain Paul Azinger put out a reminder of his own, planting a 'Bad Faldo' counter-story, one that seemed designed to undo all the Englishman's attempts at reinvention via his new persona as a media pundit. Talking to Ian Stafford of the *Mail on Sunday* newspaper, Azinger said, 'If you're going to be a prick and everyone hates you, why do you think that just because you're trying to be cute and funny on air now, that the same people are all going to start to like you?'

When the story was picked up by the Associated Press, Azinger left a message on Faldo's phone: 'This is Zinger. Well, it's already started. I don't know if you've seen it but one of those papers said

I called you a prick and that everyone from your generation hates you. Even though you pretty much are and everyone pretty much does, I have more diplomacy than that.' Faldo publicly laughed off the comments, telling *Golf Digest* that Azinger had just 'got a swift education in Fleet Street'.

However, Faldo's tone with *The Times* suggested he viewed the 'prick' comment anything but accidental: 'Paul's telling everyone that he goes with the flow, and yet he's changed the points system, changed the number of picks, changed the foursomes to fourballs. He is monitoring everything.'

When his team subsequently lost at Valhalla, Faldo's Bad Captain story was a mirror image of Langer's Good Captain story. Where Langer was reserved and democratic, Faldo was stand-offish and his team were rudderless.

Not surprisingly, the Englishman prefers to remember his experience differently. 'You missed the bit on Sunday night,' Faldo said. 'Eventually we ended up with just the 13 of us sitting and chatting, which was great. Lee Westwood said, "Wow, this is great. We've never done this before." We just sat around for a half-hour just gassing. Westwood said, "We're all going to stay friends for this," because of the experience we'd just had. And they [Harrington and García] jokingly got up and hugged and said, "Even we'll be friends." So I take that as witnessing something for real instead of reading about it.'

Faldo lost in 2008 and his captaincy never escaped Azinger's 'prick' slur. In 2014, American captain Tom Watson battled a counter-story of his own, one that he never got beyond during the course of his captaincy. When he lost, this counter-story was the basis of his Bad Captain myth. Watson's leadership motif was his age.

The Train to Gleneagles

On a chilly and bright September morning in 2013, Tom Watson boarded a steam locomotive travelling between Edinburgh and Gleneagles. The 2014 American captain sat on the other side of a small, linen-covered table, scattered with the remains of discarded pastries and half-finished cups of coffee. On his smart blue blazer was a small gold lapel pin in the shape of the Samuel Ryder trophy, indicating the point of the journey. Watson was in Scotland for three days to promote the event and the train ride had been organised by the PGA of America and the European Tour, as part of a 'Year to Go' marketing campaign. Further down the carriage, Paul McGinley, Watson's opposite number as the 2014 European captain, was doing his bit, talking the talk with journalists, promoting Scotland as the 'home of golf' and glad-handing with sponsors and other members of the 'Ryder Cup family'.

Both men were being quizzed about more than golf. The media strategy being employed by the Tours was aimed at taking the Ryder Cup story out from the sports pages and into the lifestyle sections of the newspapers and the Sunday supplements. In addition to the two leading men, a number of 'ambassadors' had been employed to attract the non-golfing press to the event. As a result the train to Gleneagles was awash with celebrities, some more famous than others. There were actors, footballers, television personalities, retired models and a member of a boy band. There were Scottish politicians seeking independence for their country and a host of other dignitaries, sponsors, tour officials and public relations people.

Amid all of this, Watson and McGinley sat calmly answering questions that ranged from the obvious to the offbeat: will the

Americans be 'super-motivated' after the Miracle at Medinah in 2012? Is Paul McGinley worried about Rory McIlroy's form? Will Jordan Spieth be the new Tiger Woods? Do the wives choose the team's outfits? Will the players be tweeting from the course during the matches?

Journalists took the quotes and tried hard to read something significant into what had been said, seeking to find an angle that would then run as a news line on that day's blogs and in the next day's papers. This process continued for two days as the setting changed, moving from intimate one-on-ones to global press conferences and on to packed public halls, full of adoring Scots desperate to catch a glimpse of the ever popular Tom Watson in the flesh.

The captains in 2014 offered a fascinating dichotomy, highlighting a challenge faced by every leader, whether they are a teacher, a football manager, an American president or a Ryder Cup captain. Each must balance two conflicting traits: they must be the same as us yet, paradoxically, better than us. We want to relate to them – the Greeks called this *idiotes* – but we also want to know that they deserve the privileges of leadership – *metrios*. This dichotomy was the subplot to the two days of interviews with the 2014 Ryder Cup captains.

By giving Tom Watson the job, Ted Bishop, president of PGA of America was laying down a challenge to his European counterparts. 'I'll be a genius or an idiot,' said Bishop. 'It's a gamble. If we don't win people will look at us and say, "Wow, you've lost eight of the last ten and you pulled out all the stops. What are you going to do now?"' Bishop recalled reading *Four Days in July*, a book on the great man's near miss in the 2009 Open at Turnberry. 'When we lost in Wales [in 2010] I knew when we went to Gleneagles it would be 21 years since we last won on foreign soil and that Watson was the captain then, at the Belfry in 1993. I had this revelation: "Wouldn't it be great to bring Tom Watson back in 2014?"'

He said he'd put together an 85-page document about Tom Watson, the Ryder Cup and the future of the captaincy. 'I made a case that 2014 was a unique set of circumstances. We're going to Scotland and there hasn't been a player in modern-day history that's had a better record in Scotland than Tom. He's endeared himself to the people there. On the flight over in 1993, when Tom was last captain, he got up and addressed the team. He said, "We're going where they invented the game of golf, but let's remind them that we're coming from a part of the world that perfected the game." When we got off that plane, there was a feeling among everybody that Tom is our captain and there is no way we are going to lose with him as our leader. He's got one goal next year and that is to win it back. Look at the last 15 Ryder Cups. Nine have been decided by two points or fewer, seven of them by one or fewer. Could Tom help get that point or half point? He might just do that.'

The choice of Watson didn't surprise Curtis Strange, who says he'd heard 'rumblings in the background that they wanted to go with someone older'. This prompted Strange to get on the phone to PGA President Ted Bishop and make a case for another player of a previous generation, who in many American players' eyes had been overlooked for the captaincy. 'I said, "Tell me if I'm out of line but I just have to put in my two cents worth. There's a rumour you're going after an older captain, and I think Larry Nelson deserves the opportunity." Bishop said, "I appreciate it very much," but a couple of weeks later they announced Tom Watson.

There's nothing wrong with that pick. He brings respect. More than that, not locker room or strategy or speeches, he brings the age difference. He's like your grandfather: when he speaks the players will listen. He's lived such a long golf life and experienced so many things. When it comes down to the final matches on Sunday, will that make a difference? Probably not.' Curtis Strange, it turned out, was right.

Watson is one of the game's greatest players. His spectacular Ryder Cup record and his eight Major championship wins, garners him high points among today's cash rich American team. They admire him, but what was less clear, and what Watson needed to convey early in his tenure, was that he could also relate to his team, many of whom he didn't know personally.

At his press conference at Gleneagles, the first question Watson was asked was about his age. Was he too old and therefore too removed from the players? The same question was asked of Ronald Reagan when he was running for re-election as president in 1984 against Walter 'Fritz' Mondale, the Democratic candidate. The Mondale camp targeted Reagan's age as a weakness to be exploited during the televised debates. Reagan, directed by his strategist Michael Deaver, delivered a stunning riposte that changed the narrative of the election: 'I want you to know that also I will not make age an issue of this campaign. I am not going to exploit for political purposes, my opponent's youth and inexperience.' Even Mondale laughed.

Like Reagan, Watson decided to front up the issue straight away, describing a discussion he'd had at a pre-announcement meeting around the USPGA Championship. 'They said, "There might be an issue with your age. How are you going to deal with it?" My answer is that I have the experience of playing. I have the experience of being a captain. If I was a player on my team, I'd want to feel that I have that experience. I know that they know that I have the experience. I have their backs. Some of it is making sure the clothes fit, the mundane stuff. But I'm going to make every decision with the best possible information that I can get. I'll get to know the players, the caddies, they're the guys who really know their players, get to know their wives or girlfriends. Any bit of information can help. I'm going to be very thorough.'

Then Watson said something that revealed the true challenge of his captaincy. He aimed to keep the atmosphere light, he said, get the team laughing. Too often the Americans were too glum. In response, a journalist asked who the jokers in the American team were. Watson's answer was revealing. After a few moments pause, he said: 'Jason Dufner,' before adding, 'I hear he's a funny guy.' It was just one word but it seemed to speak volumes. Jason Dufner's qualities as a humorist may not be in doubt, it was just that the captain was guessing.

In the other corner, Paul McGinley had the opposite problem to Tom Watson. McGinley is a journeyman player whose record looks even less impressive when put next to his opponent. There are no Major championships, no Orders of Merit wins or victories in America, the usual barometers of a professional playing career. Given these cards, Europe's captain had little alternative but to play the '*idiotes*' card, taking every chance to emphasise his experience as a team man.

Throughout his tenure as captain, McGinley relished the position of underdog. He burnished his everyman story with references that highlighted his lower status in the game to Watson. He told of the time he asked Watson for his autograph during a tournament he attended as a university student in San Diego, and mocked his own lack of fame in the US, revealing to Irish journalist Paul Kimmage that he'd shared a lift with an American businessman who bragged of going to the Ryder Cup at Gleneagles but who then failed to recognise the European captain who was standing in front of him in the elevator.

The everyman image was supported by stories of McGinley's life as a team player: his early success as a Gaelic footballer in Dublin cut short by injury, and the role he has played in Ryder Cups and the Seve Trophy, a similar team event. 'I've been involved in five Ryder Cups, won all five, three as a player and two as a vice-captain,' said McGinley at Gleneagles for the Year to Go launch. 'I've seen the template for success. I've been riding shotgun. The way I see my job is to take the blueprint and enhance it, make it better, add my identity, improve it in ways I think will improve it. But ultimately, not to stray too far from what has worked. If it ain't broke don't fix it. I have complete freedom to change anything I want to.'

Reinforcing McGinley as the everyman was the fact that he was virtually elected to the job by the players. When it looked like the European Tour might offer Colin Montgomerie the captaincy for a second time, several leading European players took to Twitter. Luke Donald, Rory McIlroy and Graeme McDowell used their social media profile to lend their backing to McGinley.

Former Formula 1 team boss Eddie Jordan, a good friend of McGinley's, played a role in his support team at Gleneagles. In the run-up to the match he gave an interview to Kevin Garside of the *Independent* which articulated the everyman position perfectly: 'Alain Prost was a great driver, not so successful as a team boss. You can't assume that being a brilliant driver will automatically make you a brilliant leader. The same with golf. I know much is being made of Tom Watson's qualities and his career as an all-time great. Paul can't boast that. He doesn't need to. Paul is very laid-back, very thoughtful, very caring but, by God, when he wants something to happen it will happen. In his own quiet manner he gets things done. I have no doubt he will prove a great captain of this team.'

Unlike Watson, the difficult issue for McGinley was not that he didn't know the players, but that he was too close to them, too much one of the lads. This was McGinley's weak spot, and would have been the basis of his Bad Captain story had the need arisen. When the going gets tough, would he be able to take the big decisions that might jeopardise his close friendships with many of the leading players?

'Going up against Tom Watson is a formidable challenge,' said McGinley, playing the humble card. 'One of the great regrets of my career is that I never stood toe to toe with Tom Watson on a golf course. He was a hero of mine. My career never reached the heights that his did. I relish the thought of going against him. He's a formidable competitor and he will bring a lot more to the Ryder Cup, and add to the package of the American team. I have to step up to the plate, and so do the players.'

Having paid his dues, McGinley then went on the offensive. 'But I'm the captain of a very strong ship, in terms of what we've done in the past and the players I'll have available to me. I'm in a privileged position, in a way that Tom is not, that I've been riding shotgun on this decade or so of success we've had in the Ryder Cup. I've been sitting, watching, observing and educating myself. Hopefully that will mean I can make some really good decisions next year.'

Had America won in 2014, McGinley's collegiate approach to running the team would have been flipped to become a weakness.

Again, a political analogy is useful. Jonathan Powell was a senior advisor to Tony Blair's governments. He understood on a fundamental level the perils of the strong–weak dichotomy: 'Each time weak prime ministers succeed strong ones they invariably announce they are reintroducing cabinet government, but all they really mean is that they do not have the power to lead their government effectively themselves.'

Europe's victory ensured that McGinley's empathetic approach was seen as central to his more democratic, forward-looking leadership style, and it was Watson's considerable personal assets that were flipped to fit the story. Gravitas became distance, and his vast experience was just a reminder of his age. Award-winning sports writer David Walsh tweeted that he thought Tom Watson looked his age at the Saturday night press conference. 'That means he's aged ten years in 24 hours.' He was right, a fact that no spin doctor in the world could counter.

Chapter 17

The Team Spirit Correlation

From his position in the Sky television studio overlooking Gleneagles's first tee, 2016 captain Darren Clarke watched Ian Poulter leading the celebrations after the 2014 victory. Clarke was asked for a view of Poulter's role in the team. 'He would have inspired the other guys by backslapping them, hugging them and saying, "Come on!",' said Clarke. 'He would have brought real passion and he epitomises the European way of being there for each other. It's what we do and we seem to be able to form a bigger bond than the Americans.'

The excitement of the end of a sports event is never a good time to expect even-handed analysis, and Clarke's reading of events was allowed to pass unquestioned. The broader issue is whether Europe win regularly because they are 'there for each other' or whether the backslapping and banter are a result of winning and not a cause of it.

An extended period of success has encouraged the media to portray Team Europe as a golfing version of a Club 18-30 holiday, with Darren Clarke and Paul McGinley as fun-loving reps leading a rainbow coalition of national stereotypes, from efficient Germans and wacky Swedes to English yeomen and passionate Celts. The counter-argument is that the famed European team spirit is an illusion and that they feel better about themselves purely because they win more often. The Euro team spirit story has grown up over a period in which they have won 70 per cent of the time. Mike Atherton, the former England cricket captain, suggested that team spirit was 'something viewed through the rear view mirror by winning teams'. As Dow Finsterwald said to Paul Azinger, 'It helps if you can fight,' meaning that the chances of success are improved only by having better players on your team.

The underlying assumption is that a happy team will rally together to 'get the job done', being open and generous in team meetings and heading out to the course to support their teammates when their own matches are over. This take on European harmony is buttressed by tales from within the team room. European team spirit is regularly cited as the key differentiator between the warm, empathetic Continentals and the cold corporate Americans. Armed with this theory, we go in search of evidence to back it up. In the week before Medinah, the European players and their partners organised a private episode of *Strictly Come Dancing*, the television ballroom dancing show. 'I don't know whose idea it was but it was fantastic fun,' Lee Westwood told Kevin Garside in the *Independent*. 'I was told I've got good hips,' he said. 'I dance a mean cha-cha-cha, I can tell you. We split into teams. Poulter ruined our chances by introducing break dancing to ballroom. It brought the whole thing into disrepute. Martin Kaymer was hilarious, the worst by far. I've never seen someone so stiff and wooden. But Miguel Ángel Jiménez, one of our vice-captains, had that Latin beat off to a "T" and his team won it.'

The European team spirit story has been buoyed by many similar accounts down the years, but it gives an incomplete picture. There are plenty of examples of discord in the team room, suggesting that, like the captain myth, the notion of team spirit is something we attribute only after the result is known – and it's just that Europe has not lost very often. When it does, the fallout can be spectacular. The aftermath of 2008 is an example. Nick Faldo's captaincy was criticised by Graeme McDowell, among others, for lacking buzz – and the captain himself has not been shy to blame players for their performances. Faldo stirred this pot during his commentary stint at the 2014 match, when he suggested Sergio García was 'useless' in '08 due to relationship difficulties, a point that bridled the 2014 players at the post-match press conference.

The 2008 example suggests that Team Europe is not as united as we sometimes think. For example, did José María Olazábal overlook Pádraig Harrington at Medinah in 2012 because of their personal history, going back to when the pair fell out at the Seve Trophy in 2003? During a pivotal final-day singles match, Harrington questioned Olazábal's 'gardening', a reference to the Spanish player repairing pitch marks on his putting line. Olazábal was not amused by what he saw to be a fellow professional questioning his integrity and angrily picked up his ball, conceded the hole, stormed to the next tee and played the rest of the match in silence. The conspiracy theory gained traction when Olazábal was dismissive of Harrington's chances of earning one of his wildcard picks during the last qualifying event before Medinah.

Harrington shot an opening round of 64 at the Barclays event in America, encouraging reporters to ask what Harrington would need to do to make his team. 'At least a win,' said Olazábal, effectively shutting the door on the Irishman.

Colin Montgomerie's Ryder Cup career was ended by Nick Faldo's decision not to pick the Scot for the match at Valhalla in 2008. Was Faldo right to think that Casey and Poulter were the better bet? Or did he do it to protect his own record as the all-time leading points scorer on the European team?

What were Seve Ballesteros's motives for asking Miguel Ángel Martín to stand down from the team in 1997, when the player was insistent that his injured wrist had healed sufficiently to play in the match? 'That little man?' said Seve, when asked about Martín. 'He can't stop the Ryder Cup. Lawyers can only do so much. He's like a machine gunner shooting in all directions. He's trying to be a hero for a week. We would be out of our minds to change the decision.'

On the same subject, one of Ballesteros's team, the Spaniard Ignacio Garrido, said of the matter, 'It's the most unfair decision I have heard in the history of golf. I cannot like Seve's attitude on this, and if he comes and asks me my opinion I will say, "You are crazy."'

Thomas Bjørn, the Danish player, was above both Clarke and Woosnam in the rankings and was incensed by what he saw as Woosnam's lack of communication. 'I'm shocked and have totally lost respect for Ian Woosnam,' said Bjørn. 'It looks like he needs to learn how to be a captain. I don't understand the way he is handling the situation. I hadn't heard from him for six months. I have spoken to several of the players who are in the team and they haven't heard a word from Woosnam either. To be captain and not even communicate with your team at all – it doesn't give you much respect. He came into the bar at the hotel and gave me 20 seconds about Lee having won twice at the K Club. In a bar. That kind of sums it up. He can't walk up to me, tell me in 20 seconds and expect me to be happy.' The outburst so shook Woosnam that he later claimed to have asked several members of the team whether they wanted him to step down. 'I took five, six or seven of the guys to the K Club for a practice round,' said Woosnam. 'And I said to them over dinner, "I'm quite prepared to step down if you don't feel I can do the job." There was no question, they didn't want me to step down, and felt that Thomas was out of order. It was completely unanimous. It gave me a boost.' The ultimate arbiter of Woosnam's captaincy was the result, in which Europe inflicted the heaviest defeat ever suffered by an American Ryder Cup team.

Whether Europe's advantage in team cohesion is real or imagined, it assumes that the more together a team is the better it will perform. The narrative is a familiar one across sport. Journalists often ask the captain how the team is 'gelling', and look for signs that the 12 players are acting 'as a unit'. This suggests that there is a direct causal relationship between team spirit and performance, yet the evidence is sketchy if parallels with corporate life are considered. 'It's logical to think that having satisfied employees ought to lead to high performance,' wrote Philip Rosenzweig in *The Halo Effect*. 'After all, satisfied employees might be willing to work harder and longer, and might care more about keeping their customers happy. It sounds right.'

But several research studies carried out in the corporate world suggest the link between harmonious teams and performance is a fallacy.

In the 1970s the academic Barry Staw carried out a series of experiments into company performance and its relationship to team morale. Staw separated two groups of employees and set them group tasks. He then relayed back to them the results of their performance on a purely random basis. The people who were told they had done well looked back at their experience with rose-tinted glasses, telling tales of how bonded the team were, how well they communicated and worked as a unit. Then Staw told the other group that they had failed the task. This second group sounded like Team USA after Gleneagles: a cacophony of blame and name-calling.

'People generally think that teams that work together harmoniously are better and more productive than teams that don't,' said J. Richard Hackman, the Edgar Pierce Professor of Social and Organisational Psychology at Harvard University, and a leading expert on teams. 'But in a study we conducted on symphonies, we actually found that grumpy orchestras played together slightly better than orchestras in which all the musicians were really quite happy. That's because the cause-and-effect is the reverse of what most people believe: when we're productive and we've done something good together (and are recognised for it), we feel satisfied, not the other way around. In other words, the mood of the orchestra members after a performance says more about how well they did than the mood beforehand.'

Such research doesn't prove that team spirit is unimportant, just that asking the winning team for an objective judgement as to the level of cohesion in the team room is deeply flawed. Yet that's exactly the methodology used to judge the relative team spirit of Team Europe and Team USA over a period of the last 30 years or so. Armed with the 'evidence' of victory and defeat, journalists seek to backfill their analysis with details from the team room.

Faced with the happy smiling Euros, the American team room often appears to have all the warmth of an ambush. Compare Lee Westwood's missive from the European team's dancing competition to Jim Furyk's description of the American team room after they were thrashed in 2006 at the K Club: 'We look constipated, that's how the guys look, and I'm sure when they look at me, they see the same thing. Every two years, when the time comes, whether we're at home or in Europe, it's like we're all constipated. We just get too tight. Any other week, and that includes the Presidents Cup, we have more fun. Guys are on the range talking, joking, loose. But when it's Ryder Cup, everybody's mood seems to change. It's like we're going to work instead of going to the golf course. I don't know if that's why we haven't done better. It's got to be part of the reason.'

To invigorate their team, American captains have resorted to using any number of motivational levers. These have included some of the big ones – patriotism, religion, money – in addition to some at the other end of the team-building spectrum, such as presidential speeches, Michael Jordan videos and table tennis with Matt Kuchar.

Paul Azinger fears the American search for team spirit is a mistake. 'I didn't want to be the captain that went into the Ryder Cup under the assumption that the Americans needed to have more fun,' says Azinger. 'There is no shortcut to success – you have to prepare to play well in this event as much, if not more so, than you do in any other. Winning a golf tournament is never fun when you're in the process of trying to complete the task. The fun happens afterwards. Ask Justin Rose whether he had fun during the last round at the US Open. I guarantee he wasn't having fun until it was over. There's nothing fun about the process.'

Bob Rotella says the idea that the European players are better team men is 'a bunch of baloney': 'I've heard people say it many times but I don't think there is any real substance to it. If you are in the locker room on Tour there's no way that you would say there is any difference between American and European players in the way they interact with each other. And most of the European team plays over here anyway. Most American players are going to go to dinner either with their wife and kids or with another couple. If they don't have their families with them they go out in groups of three or five, and I think that's exactly how it is with the European players. It's not like the Europeans are poor and the Americans are wealthy, so they fly around in private jets with their family as opposed to going in coach class. The message from both Rotella and Azinger is: win and the fun will follow.

Go back a couple of generations and American team spirit is there for all to see. For a glimpse of what life was like in the American team room in the good old days, we only need to listen to Johnny Pott, who played in the 1967 American team which thrashed Great Britain and Ireland 23½ to 8½ in Houston, Texas. This remains the biggest winning margin in the event's history. It followed three similarly one-sided affairs in 1961, '63 and '65, a period of complete American dominance.

In Houston Team USA boasted Arnold Palmer, Billy Casper and Doug Sanders, and was led by one of the iconic figures of American golf, Ben Hogan. Years later, Johnny Pott recalled Hogan's pre-match team talk: 'He said, "Boys, there's nothing to being the captain of the Ryder Cup. You guys are all great players. Pairing is real easy. I'm going to pair together you boys who drive crooked. I'm going to pair together you boys who drive straight. And the first ball's going to be hit by Julius Boros because he don't give a shit about anything. So y'all just go play your game. You got these uniforms here,' continued Hogan. 'If you don't like the way they fit or whatnot, don't wear them. I never could play in somebody else's clothes. Sanders, if you want to come out here and dress like a peacock, that's fine. Whatever you want." Then Hogan paused to let the laughter subside before revealing the hammer in his pocket, making a point that wasn't lost on anyone in the room. 'But let me tell you boys one thing,' he said in his familiar Texas drawl. 'I don't want my name on that trophy as a losing captain.' Not much sign of constipation there.

Faith v Doubt. Faith One Up

Few things divide the teams more clearly than their attitudes to formal religion. Both teams have always contained people for whom faith is a central part of their lives. However, the rise of the evangelical right in American politics and cultural affairs offered the British media, in particular, the perfect chance to create a new archetype.

During the Friday afternoon fourball matches at Medinah in 2012, the American pair of Webb Simpson and Bubba Watson meted out a thrashing to the European partnership of Paul Lawrie and Peter Hanson. The Americans were 6 up through the first ten holes before closing out the match 5 and 4 on the 12th hole. The match ended with the usual pleasantries, as the four players shook hands and the defeated team made their way from the green, allowing the winners to indulge in some celebratory high fives with themselves and their two caddies. They were then joined on the green by the two players' wives, who formed a six-person huddle to share a moment in quiet prayer. Simpson and Watson were just two of several born again Christians who made Davis Love's team for Medinah, a group which also included Matt Kuchar and Zach Johnson.

This type of open demonstration of faith has become part and parcel of watching American sports, where it is now commonplace for a player to sign the cross as they run onto the pitch, or to glance upwards in prayer on making touchdown or hitting a home run. 'I think God wants you to be a winner in life, and that spills over into athletics,' said the Rev Jerry Falwell. 'If kicking butts is part of it, that's part of it. Jesus was no sissy. If he played football, you'd be slow getting up after he tackled you.' Golf's Christians are high-profile evangelists at a time when the number of people attending church in the US is falling. There are fewer believers in America, but a higher proportion of them are evangelical about their beliefs. Between 2001 and 2006 the number of evangelical 'megachurches', defined as having a weekly attendance of 2,000 or more, doubled to 1,210, giving them a combined congregation of nearly 4.4 million.

Religion's role in the Ryder Cup became supercharged at the 1999 'Battle of Brookline'. Like Kiawah Island eight years previously, the golf was pushed to the margins in favour of a more controversial theme. On the 17th green on the final day, Justin Leonard holed a long putt to effectively win the match, sparking off premature celebrations by the American team and its supporters. With Leonard's opponent José María Olazábal still to putt for a half, a crowd of players, caddies and wives ran onto the green to engulf Justin Leonard. This angered the Europeans, who felt it not only went against the spirit of the Ryder Cup matches but also interrupted their man's concentration, who still had a putt to halve the hole. A television microphone was put in front of Sam Torrance, the European vice-captain, who was sitting next to the green. His quote was a gift for the journalists watching in the media room: 'It's one of the most disgusting things I have seen in my life. Tom Lehman calls himself a man of God, but his behaviour has been disgusting today.'

Torrance's quote had positioned Tom Lehman as the preacher in chief of American golf, particularly when the player was made captain for the 2006 match at the K Club in Ireland. Journalists noted Lehman's wrist bracelet inscribed with the letters W. W. J. D. ('What would Jesus do?'). Lehman is just one of several leading American players whose religious faith has come to define them in the eyes of European golf fans and the media. When Corey Pavin, another born again Christian, captained the Americans in 2010, three of his four discretionary wildcards were men of faith and fellow members of the PGA Tour's weekly Wednesday evening Bible classes: Stewart Cink, Zach Johnson and Rickie Fowler. 'The messages aren't really Bible study so much as inspirational, on topics like courage and patience,' Paul Azinger told the *Wall Street Journal* in 2010. 'It's non-denominational, very comfortable, very easy, and anyone is welcome – wives, caddies, media people, guests, anyone who wants to come. One thing it's definitely not is an outreach thing.'

Some Europeans seem to find this type of account difficult to balance, though. Instead they accuse golf's evangelicals of hypocrisy, of using God as a way of justifying to themselves their extravagant lifestyles: taking comfort from the love of Christ *and* playing the game for enormous sums of money.

The preacher archetype by turns amuses and irritates some players and fans on the European side of the Ryder Cup divide. There is hypocrisy on both sides of this debate, of course. In their rush to mock or vilify Tom Lehman and the PGA Tour prayer group, Europeans seem capable of looking beyond their own use of faith as a prop.

At Medinah, Europe's players took inspiration from their own – secular – talisman: the great Spanish player Severiano Ballesteros, often referred to as the team's spiritual leader, who captained Europe to victory in 1997 and played in the event eight times. Ballesteros died aged 54 in May 2011, after a protracted period of illness. European captain José María Olazábal, his friend and most famous playing partner, had arranged for the Seve logo to be sewn onto his team's tribute uniform of navy jumper, trousers and white shirt. Speaking before the round, Justin Rose had said of Seve, 'He's been an inspiration for this team all week long and who knows, if something crazy happens today, I know that we are going to be looking upwards.'

Alongside hero worship, golfers of both teams have embraced the cult of positive thinking fully and without question, and Ryder Cup golfers have been every bit as evangelical as Tom Lehman in using their platform to preach its benefits.

This new religion doesn't mention sin, and has little to say about those traditional whipping boys of the Christian right, abortion and homosexuality. 'Gone is the threat of hell and the promise of salvation,' wrote Barbara Ehrenreich in *Smile or Die*. 'Positivity is not so much our condition or mood as it is part of our ideology – the way we explain the world and think we ought to function within it.' It's a description that has come to fit golfers from both sides of the Atlantic.

In 1953, *The Power of Positive Thinking* outsold every book bar the Bible. Its author, Norman Vincent Peale, targeted America's growing tribe of travelling salesmen, the road warriors of fifties corporate America. The book was aimed squarely at the 'lonely man in the motel room' who was searching for answers from a life that Peale described as 'nomadic, endlessly mobile . . . aware that every transaction was an individual performance and personal challenge'. The book's central message was that by 'changing your thoughts you change your world', the compelling notion that any fact facing us is not as important as our attitude towards it. *The Power of Positive Thinking* helped spawn a multibillion dollar industry devoted to self-improvement, or self-help. Peale is in many ways the godfather of the sports psychology industry too, the founding principles of which were articulated in *The Power of Positive Thinking*. Today, athletes talk openly of their desire to remain 'in the moment', and of the importance of approaching a challenge with a 'positive mindset', banishing negativity or scepticism.

'Anybody can do just about anything with himself that he really wants to and makes up his mind to do. We are all capable of greater things than we realise,' wrote Peale. Approaching challenges with a positive, 'can-do' attitude, thought Peale, is the key to happiness. Professional golfers shared a number of characteristics with the travelling salesmen in Peale's target market. Both were cut off from the herd, living a life of almost permanent exile in hotels, airports and drive-ins. 'As much as anyone in the corporation, salesmen face a life of constant challenge,' wrote Peale, 'in which every day is a test likely to end in rejection and defeat. But however wounded, the salesman has to be prepared to pick himself up and generate fresh enthusiasm for the next customer, the next city, the next rejection.'

It's a description that is readily understood by golfers around the world, who see themselves as artisans plying their trade on the Tours. 'Golfers are lonely,' says Dr Bob Rotella, the sports psychologist and author, who acknowledges that there is a direct line between Norman Vincent Peale and his own work with players on either team. Rotella has been a regular presence on Tours since the late 1970s and wrote his own best-selling self-help book that took the essence of Peale's ideas and reworked them for a golf-playing audience. Published in 1995, *Golf is Not a Game of Perfect* is one of the best-selling golf books of the last 20 years. He has also worked with a number of the team captains, and his absence was noted by losing captain Davis Love at Medinah in 2012. 'I do wonder why we played differently on Sunday,' said Love. 'We planned everything – except we didn't plan on being four points ahead going into that final day. I had been consulting with sports psychologist Bob Rotella leading up to the Ryder Cup [Rotella had been employed elsewhere, by the University of Kentucky basketball team]. Coach John Calipari had Bob with him throughout Kentucky's title run last season and, looking back, I wish I would've done the same. On Saturday night as I headed back from the media room to address the team, I found myself wondering, "So, we're four ahead, what do I say when I walk back in there?"' The subtext to Love's statement was clear enough: Dr Bob would have had an answer.

Golf Spreads The Message

If you were to create a new religion, professional sport would be a great way to spread the word. Televised golf has the ability to carry subliminal messages to the masses via its huge global audience, reaching people at a moment when they are fully engaged and emotionally open. Golfers, in particular, have proved outstanding spokespeople for positive thinking. Every post-round interview and press conference is a small taster course in magical thinking, in which players talk only of 'the positives' and are trained to avoid any answer that hints at introspection. The message is the same one parents drum into their kids as they pack them off to school, and upon which most management training is now based: you can be anything you want to be. It is the perfect message for our times: democratic and universal, and able to spread like a virus. It works because we are open to its promise of making us the person we want to be, that one we sometimes glimpse but who never quite stays around long enough to be of any use.

Why golfers are particularly open about their use of sports psychology puzzles Dr Rotella, who is employed by sports teams of the NFL, Major League Baseball and NBA. 'It just gets more publicity in golf. Players are more open to talking about it than in those other sports. Golfers get paid directly on how they perform, and this might lead them to be more interested in it. Another theory is that golfers are more educated, or that golf is a more mental game. I don't hold much faith in these arguments. I worked with LeBron James, and I promise you that if you play against LeBron James you will find that basketball is a very mental game. Or if you are batting against a pitcher throwing a 100 m.p.h. ball, you tend to be focused on the task ahead of you.' Likewise, tennis players often use a psychologist, but they prefer to work exclusively with one practitioner. 'It's probably because tennis is matchplay and they don't want you to give an advantage to their rivals. If golf was all matchplay, the players wouldn't be as understanding of someone like myself who works with many different players and their fellow competitors. In medal play they are comfortable because they play the course and the conditions and the score.'

High-profile sports have played a big role in normalising the language of psychology, says Dr Rotella. He watches the post-round press conferences and notes how prevalent is the use of the language of positive thinking such as being 'in the moment', or the phrase 'process orientation', for example. There are parallels between sports psychology and religion, he says. 'You could call it meditation, or narrowing the focus of the mind. All are part of the pursuit of a quiet mind.'

Critics of positive thinking are not criticising happiness. To be happy is a great thing to be, it makes us healthier and live longer. The negative side of positive thinking includes the loss of the ability to think critically, to make decisions based on a rational summing up of the evidence. It can also push the responsibility for decision-making on to a third party, whether that is God, or a swing coach.

Today's professional golfer travels with an entourage of support professionals, each of which offers consolation to a particular problem, whether that fault is in the swing or the mind. Despite the growth of the positive thinking movement in America, the country remains one of the unhappiest places in the world. Americans account for two-thirds of the global market for antidepressants, the most commonly prescribed drug in the

United States. The Happy Planet Index ranks America 150th among the world's nations. 'The social pressure to appear happy makes it even harder to deal with negative emotions and feelings when they occur. We feel guilty for feeling sad,' writes Ehrenreich.

The team spirit story is a by-product of the same flawed thinking that we apply to the Good and Bad Captain. Once we know the result it is very difficult to come to a rational account of why the success happened. We divide the teams into the Good Team and the Bad Team, based on a combination of national stereotype and other biographical details that are shaped according to the result. For example, the diverse national backgrounds of the European team can be presented as a positive trait if they win or a negative one if they lose. When they win, raised voices in the team room can be shifted in tone to become 'an honest exchange of views', presenting the team's spirit as strong enough to withstand open and frank criticism from within.

Chapter 18

The Wild One

The wildcard is some player. He wins more games than he loses and regularly makes a greater contribution to his side's performance than those who played their way onto the team by right. The wildcard's win-to-loss ratio is better than some of the greats of the game, including Tiger Woods, Phil Mickelson, Davis Love or Sandy Lyle, among many others. Yet his role in the team goes beyond points: he is the most tangible demonstration of a captain's philosophy, ambition and nerve. More than any other factor, the selection of the wildcard helps answer the question facing every captain: what type of leader am I?

By studying the wildcards over an extended period, questions emerge as to strategy and even the personality of the captain. Where does his faith lie? How much does he trust the team that has been handed to him via the money lists and the world rankings? Is he willing to blood younger players to invigorate the team room, or will it be a place for the classic Ryder Cup archetype, the Gnarled Veteran? After all, what's the point of experience if it is experience of losing,' said Davis Love at Medinah, echoing Mark James's quote from over a decade before at Brookline in 1999: 'In my experience, experience is overrated.' Maybe he will enjoy handling the 'big personalities' like Monty and Mickelson – butting into his team talks, double-guessing his every move – or he might prefer the quiet efficiency of a Steve Stricker, the 'silent assassin' from Rock County, Wisconsin?

Beyond any philosophical dimension, a full understanding of the nuts and bolts of Ryder Cup selection requires several spreadsheets and a dose of Ibuprofen. The Europeans have had discretionary picks since 1979, and the Americans were given this flexibility a decade later, after back-to-back home and away defeats in 1985 and 1987. For the match at Gleneagles in 2014, both captains were able to choose three players to augment the nine who qualified automatically according to their world ranking and performances on their relative Tours. The number of wildcards available to the captain has varied over time. José María Olazábal had just two selections to make for the 2012 match against the United States at Medinah, when he selected Nicolas Colsaerts and Ian Poulter. Olazábal's counterpart Davis Love had four picks, the legacy of changes made to the American team selection process in 2008 by Paul Azinger. Tom Watson, the 2014 captain, reverted to three and would have preferred to have no picks at all, meaning all 12 players would have had to qualify on merit rather than through the captain's patronage. 'That's what we should go back to,' said Watson, a year on from the event. To him there was something deeply un-American about wildcards. The money list was the meritocratic dream of the founding fathers, whereas the wildcards are a sign of weakness, a bailout. The picks are Obamacare.

For the European team, the process is more complicated still. Of the nine automatic qualifying places available for the 12-man team, four are taken from the European Tour's own points list and five players are selected from a different 'world points' list, based on the world rankings. The European points list comprises points (1 point equals 1 Euro) gained by players from all the European Tour's Race to Dubai tournaments during the qualification process. The world points list comprises official world golf ranking points gained in sanctioned tournaments around the world during qualifying. This is significant because it allows European players who make their living mainly on the PGA Tour to qualify for the Ryder Cup.

The home captain sets up the course and chooses the order of play. Traditionally the match started with foursomes until Seve Ballesteros switched to the less complex fourballs on the first morning at Valderrama. Ever the traditionalist, Ben Crenshaw went back to foursomes in 1999 only for Torrance to switch again three years later, a tactic aimed at putting his players at ease on that nerve-racking first morning. 'If you start with foursomes, it's such a difficult format, it can so easily go wrong,' says Torrance. 'Fourballs is simple. It's a birdie fest, go for it.'

Foursomes, or alternate shot, take up a lot of the captain's planning time and can impact greatly on the wildcard picks. Curtis Strange picked Scott Verplank specifically with foursomes in mind. 'Gutsy guy. Accurate. Tough guy. Very consistent, team player,' says Strange. 'That definition has changed a little bit over the years actually, because they are all hitting it so far. You put two bombers together and they go and play. I get that. But I like a reliable hitter in there too. Lanny Wadkins jumps out as the type you want. Look at the way he's made up. Tough guy, a bit arrogant, a bit of swagger.' Wadkins's reputation as a matchplayer is well earned. In 1993, Wadkins wound up the Europeans and he wasn't even playing. On the first tee of the Corey Pavin–Peter Baker match, Wadkins wandered over and massaged his teammate's shoulders, saying loudly enough for Baker to hear, 'This is gonna be a walk in the park.' (It wasn't.)

'That's not the type of guy I want to hang around with a lot, but I want him on my team,' says Strange. 'Scott Hoch is the same. Tough, bit lippy. You may not go to dinner with him a lot, but you want him on the team. He'll be OK in the locker room, but he'll be great on the course.'

Lanny Wadkins and Tom Watson were the first ever American wildcards, selected by Raymond Floyd at the Belfry in 1989. Floyd would not be the last captain to opt for experience over potential, and in Wadkins he had a man with a reputation as the classic Ryder Cup street fighter with a brilliant short game – that was seen as more important to his captain than form. Wadkins went into the match having missed six of the previous eight cuts in tournament golf. He was paired with Payne Stewart in the first morning's foursomes, beating Howard Clark and Mark James one up, due in no short measure to a glorious chip across the green to eagle the 575-yard 17th. By the end of the match, Wadkins was 2–2–0, beating Nick Faldo in the singles, although the match had been decided before his point counted.

By comparison, Tom Watson had struggled in his previous appearance as a Ryder Cup player. Watson played well on the first morning to keep his partner Chip Beck in the foursomes match against Ballesteros and Olazábal, a game that ended all square. The veteran American was then sent out against the same opponents in the afternoon, this time with Mark O'Meara.

The result was a thrashing, with the Spanish pairing beating Watson and O'Meara 6 and 5, including a run of scores that read 2–3–2–3 through the start of the back nine.

This European win appeared to back up the hunch of Tony Jacklin, who picked Howard Clark as one of his own wildcards. Clark and James went on to beat Wadkins again, this time with Freddie Couples in tow. Jacklin's other selections were the German player Bernhard Langer, who failed to score a single point over the course of his three matches, and Christy O'Connor, the Irishman who famously beat Freddie Couples at the last. On the final fairway, O'Connor the wildcard was given a pep talk by his captain. 'Tony Jacklin said to me, "If you put him under pressure, I promise you will win the hole and the match. Just have a good swing." And that's all I thought about. I had a big 2-iron, I made a good turn, and just hit it.' O'Connor hit his 2-iron from 240 yards to within three feet of the hole and, as Jacklin predicted, Couples wilted, carving a much shorter shot with an 8-iron to the right of the green. 'Your stomach never stops churning,' said Couples later. 'It lasts all day long. Anyone who tells you they're not nervous is lying.'

Floyd's wildcard picks, Watson and Wadkins, had contributed a combined tally of just 1½ points out of five over the first two days. Both won their singles matches playing at numbers ten and 11 respectively, so their points came too late. The Cup had already been retained due to O'Connor's famous 2-iron.

Two years later the American captain again went with conservative choices, when Dave Stockton became the first of several to ignore the considerable claims of John Daly, who had won the USPGA Championship a fortnight earlier. Stockton went with the tried and trusted pairing of Raymond Floyd and

Chip Beck. Daly is one of the great losses to Ryder Cup golf, the ultimate risk candidate. He missed out again four years later when Lanny Wadkins picked Curtis Strange from outside the top 50 over Daly who won that year's Open Championship. The most colourful and controversial figure in American golf of the last two decades remains the only player to win two Majors and not make his country's Ryder Cup team.

Three-time European captain Bernard Gallacher followed his philosophy that rookies should have to play their way onto the team. Gallacher picked Nick Faldo, Mark James and José María Olazábal. Olazábal paired with Seve Ballesteros to win 3½ points out of four over the first two days, and Mark James won a creditable two points from five matches. Faldo was pointless until the Sunday singles, when he won over Floyd in a battle of the wildcards. Chip Beck lost twice on the first day and didn't reappear until Sunday, when he beat the world number one Ian Woosnam 3 and 1.

By the mid-nineties, the imbalance in the selection processes of the two teams was beginning to become a talking point – but it wouldn't be until 2008 that any fundamental changes would take place. The American side was picked from points accumulated over a two-year period, whereas the European points system favoured the second year of qualification, which some felt put a greater emphasis on form, giving the Euros an unnecessary advantage.

In 1993, Gallacher lost for the second time in succession, this time to Tom Watson. The likeable Scot again went for the tried and trusted over experimentation. His picks were uncontroversial, as neither Seve Ballesteros nor José María Olazábal had made the team by right, and Gallacher was hardly going to leave out the most successful pairing in Ryder Cup history, despite the former's extraordinary talent showing signs of slow decline. Both players lost their singles matches, which undermined the European fightback on the final day. The other pick was Joakim Haeggman, who became the first Swede to play in the Ryder Cup, and won his singles match against John Cook, one of only three European victories on the final day, which was a major contribution to their defeat.

America again went with experience over exciting younger talent. Tom Watson balanced the four rookies who had qualified with Floyd and Wadkins, who equalled Billy Casper's record of 20 Ryder Cup victories, putting him joint-second to Arnold Palmer in the all-time list of points scorers for America. In 1995, America went into Oak Hill looking for three wins in a row and the match went down to the final holes on Sunday, with the wildcards playing pivotal roles. Coming back from two down, Faldo reached the 18th green against Curtis Strange, who lost three from three starts, leading to a classic Bad Captain story for American leader Lanny Wadkins, who was then asked to justify his leadership after his team surrendered the lead they held going into the final day. At that point it was only the fifth time in the event's history that a side had overturned a deficit going into the singles matches.

As the nineties came to an end, the matches had reached new levels in terms of media and fan interest, adding to the pressure on the teams and the captain. Future winning American captain Paul Azinger gave an early insight into his thinking when he summed up the Europeans' team selection: 'You don't need depth for this. They just put out their eight show horses.' He had noted how hard Jacklin, Gallacher and subsequent captains had worked the big dogs of European golf: Ballesteros, Faldo, Lyle, Woosnam,

Olazábal and Langer. But there were signs that some of these great players were beginning to wane and a period of transition was happening, where the next generation of European players were given greater responsibility.

Winning can be misleading. It encourages over-confidence and leads to bad decisions. The bubble of team spirit can throw a mantle over problems that should be addressed. This is often the reason that great teams fall into decline and sporting dynasties end. When companies succeed, the people in charge conclude that their own talents and the current business model was responsible, and tend to discount external factors. Maybe this is what happened to Team USA? Perhaps they failed to ask the difficult questions in the good times and to master the difficult task of learning from success. The wildcards are a microcosm of this issue. A winning team suggests that all is well, just as on an individual level, past form and a big reputation can be a trap. Big names are also an insurance policy against future criticism.

How can you not pick Seve Ballesteros? Or Nick Faldo? Who would be brave or dumb enough to leave out Tiger Woods, or Colin Montgomerie? Ian Poulter is a shoo-in. Isn't he?

In 1993, Seve Ballesteros's back was becoming a worrying issue for Bernard Gallacher. It was unlikely to last five series of matches, meaning the captain would have to break up the famous Seve and Ollie double act that had proved so successful in the past. He didn't, and they lost as a pair for the first time since 1987, going down in the foursomes to Tom Kite and Davis Love. Ballesteros took the decision out of Gallacher's hands the following day when he withdrew from the afternoon fourballs. His caddie Billy Foster recalled that afternoon in the book, *How We Won The Ryder Cup*: 'In total contrast to 1991, Seve couldn't hit a cow's arse with a banjo. He'd gone. His confidence was low . . . too many swing thoughts . . . Only Seve's magnificent putting and José's sheer determination to get something out of their matches kept them winning.' Two years later, Ballesteros was again a shadow of the player that lit up the world stage in the 1980s, to the extent that Gallacher was forced to put him out first in the Sunday singles against Tom Lehman 'because you can't lose us the Ryder Cup from that position, Seve'.

Ian Poulter confirmed his place in Ryder Cup history by being the only player to boast a perfect record as a wildcard pick. Poulter has done this twice, at Valhalla and Medinah. In 2012, in his fourball match with Rory McIlroy, Poulter made five consecutive birdies to win the match on the last hole. The Englishman's role was summed up by 2014 captain Paul McGinley, when he said that his performance on Saturday afternoon at Medinah was one of the most remarkable moments he had seen in sport, comparing it to Liverpool's comeback in the UEFA Champions League final in 2005.

Poulter's Medinah heroics caused a problem for McGinley. The idea of the Englishman not being picked seemed absurd. In the decade since his debut in 2004, Poulter had evolved into the team's talisman, continuing a story begun in 1983 by Seve Ballesteros at Palm Beach. 'I'm one of those players who stands tall,' said Poulter in the week running into 2014, talking with the confidence of a man boasting an 80 per cent win record. 'When I do that and when I hole putts and am seen showing the emotion, I guess that can be the intimidation factor.'

McGinley picked Poulter as a wildcard over Luke Donald, and victory saved the captain from further explanation – despite the talisman making just one point from his three matches after a 5 and 4 fourball drubbing with rookie Stephen Gallacher on the first morning. If Europe had lost in 2014, McGinley's selection of Poulter would have been his weak spot, used as evidence against him. Rather than the team's talisman, Poulter would have swiftly moved into the category of captain's indulgence, of over-reliance on past performances and an indicator of over-confidence in Team Europe following back-to-back (but very narrow) victories.

Chapter 19

Time for a New Story

Phil Mickelson looked out at the audience of golf writers and TV crews packed into the temporary structure in the grounds of the Gleneagles Hotel. Very soon the faces and the cameras would swing his way. This was Mickelson's eighth loser's press conference at a Ryder Cup, the eighth time he would be asked to explain the troubled recent history of Team USA.

It was no secret that the player was unhappy with the way he had been treated by captain Tom Watson over the previous 72 hours. Paired with Keegan Bradley, Mickelson had won a point in the first morning's fourball matches against the strong pairing of Sergio García and Rory McIlroy. This was followed by defeat in the afternoon at the hands of Graeme McDowell and French debutant Victor Dubuisson, a loss that prompted Watson to drop Mickelson and Bradley for the entire second day, despite the pair's stellar record of four wins and one draw in five matches together going back to Medinah in 2012. It was the first time in ten Ryder Cup appearances that Mickelson, 44, had sat out an entire session.

The Saturday evening team meeting had gone badly. 'You stink at foursomes,' said Watson to his team as he entered the room. Later, the team gave Watson a gift in the form of a replica of the Samuel Ryder trophy, the kind of well-meant gesture common through the history of the event. Watson didn't seem to appreciate the present and his offhand reaction irritated Mickelson and others, fuelling the whispers of disharmony in the camp.

Prompted by a question from an American journalist, Mickelson framed his analysis of the 2014 match through the lens of a captain myth of the recent past. He recalled Paul Azinger's leadership at Valhalla six years previously, the sole American victory in more than a decade. 'Unfortunately, we have strayed from a winning formula in 2008 for the last three Ryder Cups, and we need to consider maybe getting back to that formula that helped us play our best.'

Shortly after Team USA left the press room, the victorious Europeans entered stage right, led by last-putt hero Jamie Donaldson, who was riding the Danish player Thomas Bjørn piggyback, beer in hand. The questions to the Europeans were broadly the same as those to Watson, Mickelson and Team USA: why does Europe keep winning? The answers again placed the captain at the heart of the story.

Paul McGinley's captain myth was that of the meticulous schemer, the product of the 'boot room', a kitchen cabinet of former and future captains at the heart of Team Europe's enduring success.

'I think Paul had a great template and a model for captains going forward,' said Lee Westwood, a veteran of Team Europe since making his debut at Valderrama in 1997. Buoyed by that day's victory, Westwood went further, coming very close to suggesting McGinley had found a definitive method – the answer – as to how to win the Ryder Cup. 'I think you could base your captaincy and your future captain around the way Paul did it this week,' said Westwood, to nods from some of his teammates alongside him behind the press conference desk.

The media's accounts of McGinley's captaincy were of a similar flavour, peppered with words and phrases such as 'attention to detail', 'empathy' and 'planning'. Veteran golf writer John Hopkins wrote that Tom Watson had been 'out-captained by Paul McGinley . . . a man whose meticulous preparation set a new standard for Europe captains'.

Rory McIlroy was more specific in his praise: 'From the first day we got here, the speeches that he gave, the videos he showed us, the people that he got in to talk to us, the imagery in the team room, it all tied in together; all part of the plan, all for the cause of trying to win this Ryder Cup.'

This was the euphoria of victory talking – well meaning, but wrong. There is no formula, no template. This is just the captain myth at work, confusing cause with correlation and exploiting our need to tell a coherent story once the result is known. As Paul Azinger once put it, 'There have been some captains who have micro-managed everything and lost. There have been captains who were drunk every night and won. There is no blueprint on winning. He just needs to do everything he can to give the players the best opportunity to be successful, then trust your players and then get the heck out of the way.'

The craving for certainty is there in the words used by the players and the media; the language of sport has changed, encouraged by the rise of sports science, and it has bled into sports reporting. But if golf were a science, Tom Watson would have played the greatest pairing the scientific world has to offer: trial and error. Watson the scientist would conduct experiments that recreated exactly – or as close to as possible – the conditions of the match at Gleneagles on that Sunday in 2014: the same line-up against the same opposition in the same weather on greens of the same stimp reading with the same pin placements. Then he would have repeated the experiment over and over and over again until he was confident that his method – his Sunday singles line-up – was proven to be optimal. Only then would he send his troops into battle to get the necessary points required to win the Cup.

But golf isn't a natural science, and the unforgiving logic of scientific inquiry does not apply in the same way. Players are human beings. They behave irrationally. They have mood swings to add to their golf swings which, as much as some famous coaches would have us believe, are not entirely repeatable robotic actions. Even the very best golfers in the world are enhanced and ruined by such intangibles as feel, touch and intuition, which distort the data, making decision-making unreliable at best and a crap shoot at worst.

'We would love to make Petri dishes of corporations, but we can't,' wrote Jim Collins in *Good to Great*, one of the biggest-selling business books of the last two decades. 'We have to take what history gives us and make the best of it.'

Luckily for those of us who love to watch it, the Ryder Cup is brilliantly, thrillingly unpredictable, and that's how it's going to stay. Instead of scientific rigour, the captain, like all leaders, is left with a fudge: he must work with imperfect information, luck and probability.

'Once you've internalised the concept that you can't prove anything in absolute terms, life becomes all the more about odds, chances, and trade-offs,' wrote ex-US Treasury Secretary Robert E. Rubin, a former Goldman Sachs trader. 'In a world without provable truths, the only way to refine the probabilities that remain is through greater knowledge and understanding.'

The frustration at the heart of the captain myth is that the Ryder Cup should be a great model for leadership, one that sends a message that talks to the future, not the past.

The event is selling many things, some obvious, others less so. Sponsors and advertisers pay huge sums for access to an audience of tens of millions of people, turning the event into a marketing channel down which all manner of products and services are pushed – from golf clubs, shirts and shoes through to insurance, financial services and hard liquor. And that's just the start; the Ryder Cup is selling so many other things too, they just aren't labelled with logos and price tags in the same way. Many subliminal messages can be found just under the surface, from flag-waving American patriotism and European unity through to the cult of positive thinking, evangelical religion and even racial politics.

The captain's profile has grown with that of the event, meaning he too has become a valuable marketing tool in his own right. Sponsors cluster around him in increasing numbers, seeking an association with what he represents. He has become a go-to guru on managing elite performance, dealing with stress under pressure and winning against the odds. Each of these talks directly to the corporate world that is willing to pay large sums for the advice.

This has turned the winning captain into a valuable commodity – Paul McGinley is said to have earned around £2 million from media and corporate interest up to and after Gleneagles. Like any of us given this opportunity, the Good Captain is happy to take advantage, and in doing so he perpetuates the myths, ensuring that a flawed 'blueprint' of the captaincy evolves with every passing event.

Five assistant captains; cashmere sweaters; table tennis in the team room; rousing speeches and first-tee histrionics: it's a brave, or foolish, captain who tinkers with a 'winning formula', however dodgy its foundations. Anything that deviates from the norm creates fertile ground should the Bad Captain story be required. Rather than encourage innovation, the captain myth stifles it.

Very rarely do we discuss the limits of leadership. One reason for this is that it is not in the interests of the leadership industry, which earns a great deal of money from selling solutions. The truth is less easy to package and sell. Getting things done is often a slog. There is no magic bullet to performance, no one single solution. Instead, what we often mistake for leadership is actually public relations. This is as true of the captain as it is the most powerful person on earth.

'If we insist on turning leadership into messiahship, we should hardly be surprised at the president's showmanship,' wrote Elvin Lim, author of *The Anti-intellectual Presidency*, of President Obama's handling of the BP oil spill in the Gulf of Mexico in 2010. The President's ability to clear up the mess – or even to prevent such a thing happening again – is and remains very limited: he is not able to police the seas or seize company assets until they clean up the mess. Instead, President Obama, like every politician before or since, took steps to *appear* to be acting. He visited the site, he made speeches and showed empathy to the victims. Like Tony Jacklin with his walkie-talkie, Obama was leading before our very eyes.

The Rise of the Follower

The history of the Ryder Cup spans a period that has seen a revolution in the way we think and talk about leadership and the treatment of people at work. In the black-and-white days of the 1920s, when Walter Hagen and Ted Ray were teeing it up in Worcester Massachusetts, the world's leading business thinkers were men such as Frederick W Taylor and Max Weber. They were seeking management solutions to the problems of mass production, the process of making cheap products at scale. Weber and Taylor created bureaucracy, which remains the abiding management principle we live with today. It has endured for so long because it worked, albeit at a huge cost in terms of human misery for the people who worked in their factories.

The people humping stone to build the pyramids, says management expert Gary Hamel, would recognise the working practices of most modern companies. Most workplaces remain wedded to structures where power and decision-making reside at the top, disempowering the many and empowering the few. 'It concentrates the job of strategy and direction in the hands of a very few people. It gives them the ability to hold the capacity to change hostage to their own personal willingness and ability to change.'

The 21st-century business world requires a different approach. We still have to be efficient and focused, but also adaptable and creative. The leadership industry needs to tell different stories that reflect these changes in management philosophy, which in turn hold a mirror to the rise of the follower in everyday life.

Devolution is the one constant theme in management theory since 1927. 'It used to be that leaders were meant to dominate those who followed,' wrote Barbara Kellerman in *The End of Leadership*. 'Now followers are bolder and leaders are meant to persuade and recommend, not order. This shift in power can be seen throughout history with the transitions in marriage and politics – a shift away from an unequal power balance to one that is more democratic and just.'

Followers used to be 'the herd', a passive bovine presence, slow and dependent, in need of guidance. This is changing. Followers are hip. The herd mentality has shifted to the wisdom of crowds, and the team-centric nature of the Ryder Cup positions the captain as the perfect salesman for a new definition of sports leader. Using the media profile at his disposal, the captain is well placed to promote a new, more useful and relevant debate around leadership in sport and end the cult of the manager. 'The age of the all-powerful executive has ended,' wrote Kellerman. 'Followers the world over are getting bolder and more strategic – which is why many leaders who dismiss or discount them do so at their peril'.

In a bureaucratic world, the power relationships are clear for all to see: leaders are the ones at the top. When the bureaucracy is removed, the job of identifying these two groups becomes far harder. Gary Hamel posits that the ultimate test of leadership in the 21st century is whether people follow you regardless of your position in the hierarchy, and without access to the threat of sanction. Faced with these criteria, even the best paid CEOs and politicians in high office can come unstuck.

'First, assume you have no positional authority. No job title. And second, assume you have no sanctions,' says Hamel. 'If someone doesn't agree there's nothing you can do. Then ask yourself what could you get done with those two assumptions. If you can do something amazing, you are a leader. If you need one or both of those levers, we're not having a conversation about leadership, we're talking about how to be a good bureaucrat. And that's OK. But let's not pretend we're talking about leadership, because we're not.'

Something interesting happens when we apply Hamel's criteria for leadership to the captaincy. It could be a great model for modern bottom-up decision-making if only we would listen. Unlike head coaches or performance directors, the captain has no sanctions and very few trappings of office. The job is unpaid beyond expenses and the post holder often has little in the way of relevant past experience to demonstrate his suitability for the job. If he can get people to follow him given those restrictions, then he's doing something right.

Recent captains such as Olazábal, McGinley and Azinger have used the language of followership – a clumsy term, and one that has proved a hard sell but which holds the key to organisational success. The role has changed a great deal over the years, says José María Olazábal, referencing the early days of the Ryder Cup. 'At the very beginning, leadership was pretty much whatever the captain said was done – there was no interaction with players. Nowadays you must have a better idea of how to approach certain individuals in the team, and it helps to have a better interaction between the players.' Today's captains, he says, are expected to foster a supportive atmosphere in the sanctuary of the players' room. 'I'm not going to be on top of them on the golf course because every player knows their game better than I do. I cannot go there and tell a player: "Well, you have to hit a high cut shot to that flag." Maybe he feels more comfortable with a solid, straighter shot, aiming just a little bit right of the target.' To this freedom is added a layer of consultation. 'I'm going to talk to them and see how they are feeling, so that they can feel comfortable. I have found out from my own experience, in past years, that when I got to a team it was a big help if I could express myself – be myself – so the other players knew what my ideas were.'

Olazábal's understated description of the captaincy is all too rare and chimes with the picture of leadership painted by management thinker Henry Mintzberg. He too rallied against the cult of the CEO, the all-powerful and often-damaging superstar captains of industry whose salaries have grown to match their egos.

'Quiet management is about thoughtfulness rooted in experience,' wrote Mintzberg. 'Words like wisdom, trust, dedication, and judgement apply. Leadership works because it is legitimate, meaning that it is an integral part of the organisation and so has the respect of everyone there. Indeed the best managing of all may well be silent. That way people can say, "We did it ourselves." Because we did.'

Can such a nuanced and subtle leadership story exist in today's global sports media, with its need for stars and stories, triumph and disaster, attribution and blame? Almost certainly not. It's far easier to go back to the cartoons of the Good and Bad Captain, with their beguilingly simple explanations of triumph and failure. So we'll continue to use the captain as a punchbag and turn him into a false idol, and to project onto him our views, fears, prejudices and aspirations.

But the one thing we do know for sure is that the captain myth says more about us than it does about him.

Acknowledgements

The chances of my becoming Ryder Cup captain deteriorate with every passing year, so the views of the men who had done the job were an essential element of this book. These interviews took place over a period in which I was working for a variety of publications, most notably the *Wall Street Journal*, *The Financial Times*, *The Irish Times* and *Golf International magazine*. Their presence in the book does not represent their endorsement of it.

To the list of captains there are many others I want to thank for their help and generosity. Britain's greatest amateur player Peter McEvoy offered his enthusiasm and knowledge without complaint, and I thank Keith Waters of the European Tour for his patience while I quizzed him for hour upon hour at Wentworth, trying to understand how the world rankings work. Talking to Professor Gary Hamel at London Business School was an education in itself. Thanks also to Dr Bob Rotella and Professor William Hurley for their contributions. The initial idea for the book arose from the enjoyable hours spent working with the sage of the sports marketing world, Shaun Whatling.

Whenever I mentioned to anyone that I wanted to write a book, they all told me I should talk to David Luxton, the best agent in the business. So I did, and here we are. David's invaluable help led to my second stroke of luck. Writing the book brought me into the orbit of the brilliant Charlotte Atyeo, the publisher of Bloomsbury Sport. I can't thank Charlotte enough for her endless patience and good advice as she prodded and poked my random outpourings until they emerged two years later, looking book shaped.

Ian Preece's comments and skilful editing were invaluable, as was the help from Holly Jarrald and the team at Bloomsbury in London and New York.

Writing about golf has been a happy accident, encouraged by Richard Simmons, Pete Simmons and Robert Green at Golf International, and I cherish our annual adventures at The Open. My thanks also go to Peter Chapman at the *Financial Times* and Jonathan Clegg and Joshua Robinson, sports editors of the *Wall Street Journal* in London. Kevin Roberts gave me my first proper break in journalism and remains the kindest, smartest person I know in the sports business.

Jo Simmons, Steve Lowe, Jude Shard, Simon Heap and Jaine Colwill Heap will never know how much they helped to keep my spirits up with their interest, encouragement and red wine, and Martin and Suzanne Miell Ingram endured night after night of incoherent ramblings in the bars across northern Spain. To Andrew Peel, Richard Hingley, Adrian Pettett, Tony Gill, Steve Tompkins, Dave Tompkins, Colin Burles and Barry Seymour, I apologise for my golf, but thank them for a lifetime of friendship.

Often while I was writing this book I'd think of my dad, George Gillis. I wish I had the chance to talk to him about it. Mum, Lyn, Sandra, Mark and I miss him now as always.

Finally, to Penny and Olivia, without whose support – emotional, financial, editorial – this book would never have seen the light of day. You know how much I love you but it's nice to get the chance to say it publicly.

Index